THE PROFITABLE BLOGGING SYSTEM 2.0

STEP-BY-STEP ACTION PLAN TO TURN YOUR BLOG INTO A BUSINESS

Durga Thiyagarajan

Clever Fox
PUBLISHING

Chennai • Bangalore

CLEVER FOX PUBLISHING
Chennai, India

Published by CLEVER FOX PUBLISHING 2023
Copyright © Durga Thiyagarajan 2023

THE PROFITABLE BLOGGING SYSTEM OUTLINE

Dedication

"For my husband Thiyagarajan, who has always encouraged me to follow my dreams and supported me every step of the way. Your love and encouragement have meant the world to me. This book is a small way of saying thank you."

INTRODUCTION

*I*n the early morning, she logged on to her computer to check her email.

Notification from Paypal:

"You have received $1000 from XX Company PVT.ltd."

"Oh my goodness! It is working!

I am making consistent money online!

At that moment, she understood that blogging went from something she was "TRYING"…

She stood a little taller…

Held her head up higher…

She felt not only empowered but capable of doing ANYTHING.

After years of feeling stuck and broke, she took control of her life and made it happen for herself.

This is one of the most-heard stories in the online world. I have read this in most ads, blogs and emails if I am right.

Yes! This story can be yours too.

But stop!

How did you feel after reading this story?

Did it tempt you to start a blog?

Did you feel motivated and believe you could make money like her?

Or did you feel like you are the only one who still needs to make money from your blog?

If you are asking yourself

"Why am I not making progress?"

"Why am I not able to move that needle to success?"

You have tried every possible strategy, purchased many tools, and spent dollars on courses, but things need to move faster than you like.

The initial exciting mode is converted into overwhelmed, exhausted mode. You should be sure that whatever effort you put in is worth it.

Whatever might run through your mind, pause that for a minute to the reality check. Let's go…

There are around 60 million[1] blogs in WordPress alone. Only some bloggers make 5 and 6 figures income. 33% of bloggers don't earn any money.[2]

Hey, my dear reader, pat yourself! You are not the only one struck in this hamster wheel. There are too many blogs that make very little to no income.

And the reality here is - It is not as easy as you think. But when done with the right strategy and precise idea, You can make consistent earnings and build a business out of it.

The Right strategy includes,

- Choosing the **Profitable Niche** that meets all the ends.
- Creating the **Perfect content strategy**.

- Composing your **Product ecosystem** to make money from your blog.

The 3C's and the **"CONSISTENCY"** will get you the success you want. This book will help you with that.

This Book vs other Blogging Books:

There are plenty of books on Blogging and Content marketing. What makes this one different from them?

Here are the two reasons I would like to put forth.

Reason 1: You will learn the business foundation that works in 2023.

Most books, guides, and articles are outdated and sugar-coated with the latest trends that fade out in time.

They are not going to work in 2023.

What you need are the real foundations to build any business.

That is what I am going to share with you in this book.

You will have two strong foundations here as a beginner.

1. **The Learning Ladder**- There are too many things to learn when building an online business. I have curated them perfectly (stage-wise) so that you can save time and go ahead fast.
2. **The Ideal Niche Selection**- You will learn the latest method to choose the niche(the topic of your blog)without losing your sanity.

Reason 2: You will learn the Pyramid Blogging System.

You musust master content creation(writing blogs) to make money from blogging.

But it takes a lot of work to find time and write fast.

In this book, you will learn the exact methodology I use to create content for my three niche sites.

The fail-proof content writing strategy+workbook.

Few disclaimers before you go:

- For about five years, I have been using this method suggested in this book to create content for my niche sites. This method yields value when done with effort. It's possible to make a sustainable living from a blog regardless of your niche.
- For simplicity, I didn't focus on the technical setup of the blog. You have a sea of tutorials on WordPress.
- The ultimate purpose of this book is to encourage, inspire and enable you to grow your platform and take your blog to the next level.
- I fill this book with the practical takeaways and action steps behind each chapter to help you assess and create the most successful plan for your audience.
- There are so many shortcuts to make the blogging process faster and reduce the number of mistakes you make. Start implementing the techniques you read here and develop your strategy soon.
- You can work like a digital drudge to start and grow your blog, but all those hours only matter if you find a plan for success or a clear roadmap to follow. That's precisely what this book will help you with.

Let's get started!

Reality Check:

Answer me honestly before we proceed with this book. Just Ignore everything that you have read online. The method, strategy, tips and tricks throw all those things out of your mind and pause for this reality check.

There are dozens of tasks in front of you as a solopreneur. Doing correctly at the right stage will give you the success you aim for.

But most people do it wrongly and expect the results quickly. Agree or not, that's the real cause of overwhelm and getting stuck.

Here is the best solution I can offer for the initial overwhelm

- **Understand yourself** -I call this Self Mastery. Take some time to dig deeper into your skills and potential.
- **Understand the Market** - There is a connection between you and the market when building a personal brand because you will help someone who was struggling like you in the past.

These are the two things that you will learn in the next chapter.

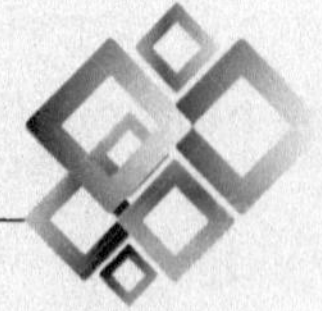

CHAPTER 1

THE LEARNING LADDER

Welcome to the New Digital Biz world!

Here you are, the business owner,

You are the employee,

You are the bookkeeper,

You are the graphic designer,

You are the content writer,

You are the video editor,

You are the social media manager,

You are "EVERYTHING"

Until you reach a point to hire someone.

Yes! You have a hefty load of tasks in front of you every day to execute.

You need to keep an eye on tracking your competitor, analyze your metrics, and create content. You have to respond to emails and social media messages. And more tasks yet to come…It's easy to get distracted when your plate is fully loaded. Someone of you might even feel, "Oh My God" is this so difficult to start and run an online business?

But Stop!

Agree or not? There is a sea of information online. There are 6 million blog posts published every day.

Most people fail because they don't know what to learn and who to trust. But don't worry. You don't need to worry about attaining goals when you can segregate and do what is needed at the right time. This is what we are going to learn in this chapter. How to learn and organize your business goals based on your knowledge and the current stage of your business. Let's talk about the learning ladder with an example in my case.

Case study - How an aeronautical Engineer turned into an entrepreneur

I am an Aeronautical Engineer. When I started blogging in 2015, I was working in a corporate. My first blog was aerostuffs.com, and I wrote about GATE exam preparation for aeronautical engineers. The blog was just a documentation of my learning process; I added pictures of my notes and explanations for solving different problems. I know nothing about SEO or organic traffic, but my inbox was full of problem requests and thanking comments. When many people approached me for GATE classes, I started Skype classes for them. This was the very first touching point on my entrepreneurial journey. I had full control over when and where I worked, leading me to create something new and innovative.

After quitting my corporate job in 2016 and getting married, I became a professional blogger. I spent lakhs on courses and ebooks to serve my curiosity to become an entrepreneur. Like others, I had often failed to reach a possession like this. After doing a professional degree in Digital Marketing and becoming V-skill certified, I started working for agencies as a freelancer while building my niche sites.

Today I have 3 successful niche sites and 1000s of students learning from me. The pleasure of being an entrepreneur is more challenging and rewarding than I describe in a few words.

It's a time-consuming process, as it often involves working long hours and making significant sacrifices. This can be particularly challenging for mothers, who may have additional responsibilities related to caring for children and managing a household. The unique challenges in balancing work and family obligations led me to find ways to delegate tasks to manage the workload effectively.

One of the mistakes I made earlier was spending too much time learning everything myself. I should have outsourced specific tasks like website design, logo creation, product design etc. That is why building a learning ladder is the first chapter of this book. The time spent on what we learn is essential and defines our success rate. The reality here is youngsters will have too much time, energy and less money. Employees/Moms will have less time, and energy. Based on your current scenario, you can choose the best path.

Comparatively, a person marketing in a firm finds this easier to do. A journalist finds it easy to publish content every day. A designer finds it easy to build a website. So the learning curve changes from person to person.

Learning differs from Person to person based on their skills

The Learning Curve

> **Fact #1: Learning curve is different for everyone, obviously the success rate also differs.**
>
> The Most important lesson here is, not to compare your success or vanity metrics(Likes, shares,comments,page views etc) with someone else.
>
> *Action step: Take a SWOT test to identify your skills and figure out what you need to learn before getting started.*

What is needed to build a One person business?

You know there are many things to do when building an online business. You will never get that satisfaction of "I have done it". It is easy to get sucked into the hamster wheel. The only solution for this is building your Learning Ladder so that you aim at the right goals. This is the best way of escaping from the information trap.

You need to do two things to build your learning ladder

1. **Self Discovery - Your State of Possession.**
2. **Skill Discovery - Skills needed to turn your passion into a business.**

One of the biggest killer is that people don't believe business is for them. Most people think that they need more experience. Believe it or not, the state of work is changing. Most things are digital here. We know that. Employers are hiring based on what content you share online. Yes, it's a new reality that we need to accept. If you have helped your family and friends with any topic you have learned, you have enough experience. Even more, how do you gain experience?

I'll tell you one thing; you only gain experience by stepping into the field. You gain experience by practising your skills in the real world.

Suppose a freelance (Web designer, artist, illustrator) can reach out to people with zero experience(to gain experience) in exchange for money. Why can't you build a business out of your content? Can't you turn your blog into a business?

Make it make sense.

Kill your imposter syndrome here - Right now!

The Route to Entrepreneurship:

We are ingrained with this corporate culture. The system is very simple. You must be in the office daily, following the manual(your routine tasks) to get the boss's approval. Complete your tasks before the deadline, and you will be rewarded.You have significantly less choice to unleash your creativity.

There is rapid learning progress at the beginning when it comes to learning corporate tasks. You acquire the skills so quickly. Upon executing the tasks daily, you reach a level where you are no longer interested in executing them. This is called a Plateau in the learning curve. It could signal that the learner has reached a limit in their ability or that a transition may occur. It could also mean that the individual has lost motivation or is fatigued.

The Corporate learning curve.

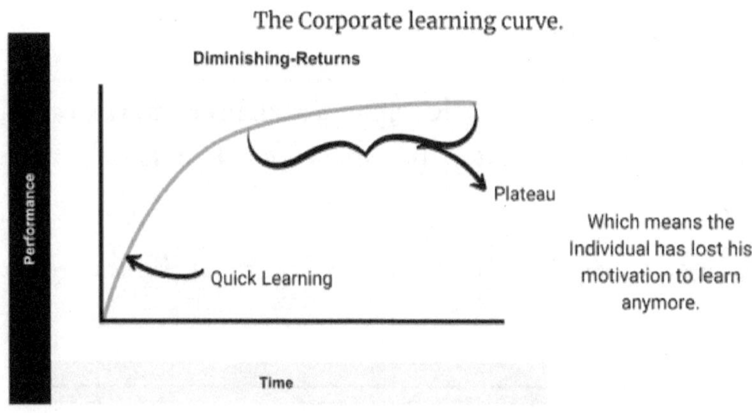

Look at the curve below.[3]

There is nothing wrong with proceeding corporate lifestyle. I am sharing this here because the learning curve for an entrepreneur is entirely different. The vital thing here is we are new to this entrepreneurial lifestyle. Schools or colleges didn't teach us anything about becoming a boss. You are responsible for every step you take. Look at the learning curve of an Entrepreneur.[4]

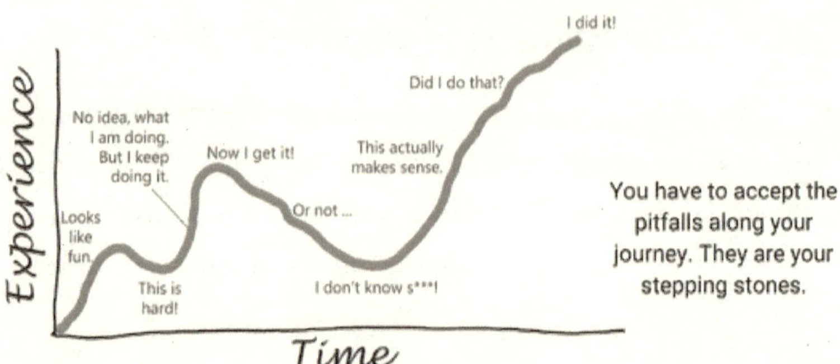

You have initial fun when you are learning. Then you will understand how complex things are. You will be frustrated with the mountain of tasks in front of you. Until you make that single dollar, you will have every stress a corporate employee has. Once you are done with finding the perfect route to earn a consistent income, everything gets aligned. You can outsource the tasks, expand your team and build a profitable business. A lot of patience is required to transform into an entrepreneur.

Fact #2: There is no shortcut to becoming a Millionaire. You are capable of adapting to this new culture. Be patient enough to figure out your strategy.

Action step: Remember this *"When the going gets tough, the **tough get going"*.- Joseph P.Kennedy*

There are two paths to building a business, depending on the individual's situation.

1. **The Fresh Start:** For people who want to learn a skill and build a business. Ex: Students, Housewives, Employees looking for a change etc.
2. **The Skill-based path:** For people who are already skilled and want to grow their organic traffic with their blogs. Ex: Graphic designer, Astrologer, Content Writer etc.

For those already skilled and seeking a side hustle, the Skill-Based path is the way to go. On the other hand, if you want to learn new skills and create an online personal brand-based business, the Fresh-Start path is perfect for you. So, which path will you choose? The decision is yours, but whichever way you go, be ready to experience the excitement, thrill, and satisfaction of building a successful business from scratch.

The task in front of you is simple, which path will you take? You will decide the route based on your skill set and current situation. By the end of this chapter, you will build the learning ladder based on that.

Self Discovery - Your State of Possession:

Almost every individual today has a gold mine of information, skill and experience. Most people reading this have gone through several Niche research worksheets and found their passion. Some might have learnt a skill they are passionate about.

This book has a workbook with detailed questions you can answer to find your passion. For example, start with writing what you are good at.

- What do you want to be known for?
- What are your goals and aspirations?
- How do you want to make a difference in the world?
- What things make you happy, and how can you incorporate them into your life?

- How much time do you have?

These are the few questions in the workbook to help you get started.

The Skill-based path:

You may be a content writer, copywriter, web designer, illustrator, Facebook ads manager, life coach, astrologer, virtual assistant or any other service-based business provider this is for you.

If you are struggling to sell your services.

Spending too much money on ads,

If you are stuck on the content hamster wheel, try new things daily.

Let's unstuck ourselves first with this five-step process.

This method is for those who are skilled and struggling. When you need more time to pursue your passions, this method will help you to catch track.

1. Find a problem that matches your passion
2. Experiment with different solutions
3. Document the process
4. Build a reproducible method
5. Share with others that want to be helped.

Skill Based Path

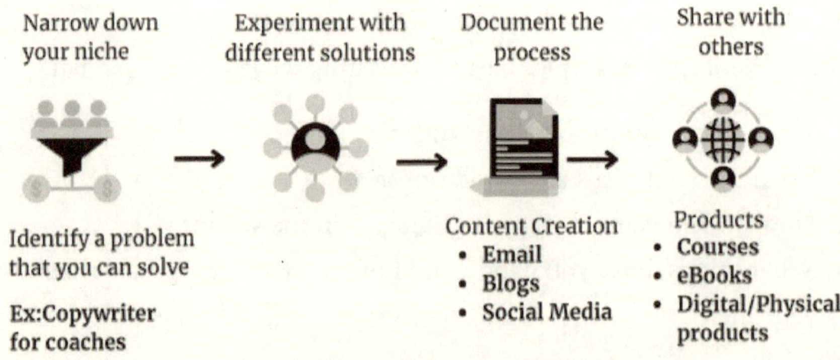

Find a problem that matches your passion:

Suppose you have already figured out your skill. You need to identify an existing problem in your niche. You can learn the process of doing this in the next chapter. I am sharing the essential things here to show you a bird's eye view of what you will learn.

Ex: If your Skill is copywriting. There are many copywriters. How can you differentiate yourself? You can narrow your idea to specific people like SAAS companies, Coaches, etc.

- Not just Copywriter - But Copywriter for Saas companies.
- Not just Copywriter - But Copywriter for Coaches.

You can define your target audience and grow your talent in that zone.

Experiment with different solutions:

You can find different strategies to grow your copywriting business for coaches.

Your strategies may include

- Creating valuable content to find clients
- You can find clients through social media
- You can find clients on various freelancer platforms.

There are so many ways to grow your business. Once you determine the best ways to earn a consistent income, you can document the entire process. To make money out of it, you have several possible routes that you can learn in the following chapters.

From corporate employee to a successful content writer: A case study of Riya's journey.

Riya was trapped in the daily grind of her 9-5 corporate job, which was her family's only source of income. Despite her love for writing, she found herself constantly stressed and yearning for an escape from the monotony of her job. That's when she decided to turn her passion for writing into a side hustle.

She identified a problem - the need for a perfect blog content writer - and started pitching to various blogs. Writing daily, she gradually built a reputation and started earning good money. As she continued exploring the possibilities, she realized she could turn this side hustle into a full-fledged business.

Riya experimented with different platforms and finally settled on Medium and other popular channels to post her content. She then took the next step and created her self-hosted blog on WordPress, pouring her heart and soul into creating quality content. Finally, she quit her job to dedicate her time fully to her passion.

But Riya didn't stop there. She documented her journey and turned it into a digital product - a course and a book. She started selling her products and continued to earn good money through her passion for writing.

Through her journey, Riya showed that turning your passion into a successful business is possible, even while juggling a demanding day job. With perseverance and a clear vision, anyone can achieve their dreams and find true fulfilment.

Meet Shweta, an ex-corporate employee turned homemaker who decided to pursue her passion for drawing

Determined to make the most of her free time, she embarked on a journey of self-discovery and found her calling in digital illustration. After enrolling in a course and honing her skills, she began sharing her work on social media and landed her first few clients. From there, she built a thriving illustration business and launched a website to sell her digital products. Now, Shweta can earn extra income doing what she loves while enjoying a fulfilling family life.

What did you learn from both case studies?

For Intellectually curious people, this content creation game is more satisfying and yields long-term results.

This career path(building a blogging business or any business out of valuable content) has complete control over how much you make, how much you work and what you work on.

In short, Omnipotent creators are those people.

- Who earn with their mind.
- Find their obsession and create masterpiece content that helps people for their betterment.
- Get paid for their compounded knowledge in the form of physical products or Digital products like ebooks, courses, templates etc.

Fresh Start - The Development-based path.

After taking multiple niche research tests, if you still need to figure out what your genuine passion is. Don't worry; it often happens to most people. This creator business is entirely new to our generation. We will figure out our passion after several failures.

Whether you are trying new, spending a lot of time in niche research, or you still need to do niche research and cope with the strategy of others and fail. Take these simple steps to find your passion. This is so important for proceeding further with this book.

1. Uncover your obsession
2. Do a Deep- Research.
3. Create Golden Nuggets.
4. Test your ideas
5. Start creating content.

"Successful people get paid for doing what they love."

What do you love to do all day? What area of your life have you improved?

Examples include - Gardening, Housekeeping, Organising, Accounting, and Self-improvement.

Some hobbies like - Drawing, Painting, illustration

Interests like - Programming, writing, designing, fitness, fashionYou have to learn to trust your gut to identify your obsession.

Take a look at your browser history; what have you watched most? (Not the Netflix shows and their reviews)

Find out what comes so naturally to you. For me, writing comes so naturally. For someone, talking comes so well.

If gardening is your passion and you have a home garden, why can't you help others build a home garden?

Development based path

Case study: How is Gayla helping people build a great garden?

Gayla is a writer, photographer, and former graphic designer with a background in the Fine Arts, cultural criticism, and ecology. Her obsession turned her into a full-time Gardener.

She is the author, photographer, and designer of best-selling books on gardening.

You can learn more about her on the blog.[5]

The Skill Discovery - The Essentials of Building an online business

To be a successful blogger, you need to wear many hats. You must have excellent writing skills that grab your audience's attention and keep them engaged. Thorough research is a must to provide accurate and informative content. Knowing the basics of SEO is essential to ensure search engines and readers find your content. Marketing your content effectively is key, including through social media and email. Analyzing your website traffic and user behaviour is crucial to make informed decisions. Time management skills are essential to publish high-quality content consistently. Building a network of contacts can help you grow your audience and gain new ideas. Creativity is necessary to come up with fresh and engaging content. And last but not least, editing and proofreading skills are required to ensure your work is polished and error-free.

Here's a list of everyday tasks of a blogger and the skills needed for each task:

1. Writing blog posts - Writing, research, creativity, editing and proofreading
2. Creating images and videos for blog posts - Image and video editing
3. Search Engine Optimization (SEO) - SEO
4. Promoting blog posts on social media - Social media marketing
5. Emailing subscribers - Email marketing
6. Engaging with readers and followers - Networking
7. Analyzing website traffic and user behaviour - Analytics
8. Managing website design and layout - Basic web design, content management systems (CMS)
9. Troubleshooting technical issues - Technical skills
10. Handling time effectively - Time management

Remember that these tasks and skills may vary depending on the type of blog and the blogger's goals. As you work towards building a successful blogging business, it's essential to prioritize your time and focus on developing your skills individually. Depending on your availability, it may not be possible to tackle all of the tasks at once. Start by identifying the areas where you already excel and build on those. Then, place the areas that need more development and start working on them one by one.

For example, if you're already a skilled writer but need to work on SEO, focus on learning the basics of SEO first. Once you have a solid understanding, move on to the next skill. By stacking your skills in this way, you can evolve your abilities inside out and build a strong foundation for your blogging business. Remember, Rome wasn't built in a day, so be patient with yourself and keep working towards your goals one step at a time.

The Learning Ladder:

Imagine embarking on a journey to build your successful blog without a map or guide. You might progress, but you'll likely wander, making wrong turns and backtracking. It's frustrating, time-consuming, and demotivating. However, with a learning ladder, you can avoid this scenario and chart a clear path to your destination. A learning ladder is a roadmap that outlines the skills you need to learn and the milestones you should aim to achieve, month by month, as you build your blog. It's like a personalized curriculum catering to your needs and goals. Following the learning ladder will save time and energy and enhance your blogging skills and confidence. You'll learn to write compelling content that resonates with your readers, design an attractive website that reflects your brand, optimize your content for search engines, and promote your blog via social media and email. You'll also track your progress, measure your success, and adapt your strategies as needed. With a learning ladder, you'll have a sense of direction and purpose and enjoy the journey as much as the destination. So, are you ready to climb the learning ladder and reach new heights as a blogger?

FYI, If you want to learn illustration, you can write in-depth skills based on what tools you will learn in the skills needed column.

Example: Illustration - Learning time 3 Months - Course details - Skills needed - Adobe Illustrator, Drawing, understanding colour palette etc.

Month	Phase	Milestone	Skills Needed	Hurdles	Revenue/Month
0-3	Learing Phase	Finding your genuine Interest	Research, Learning, Note taking	information abundance	–
3-6	Learning Phase	Finding Your Unique Perspective	Critical thinking. Problem solving, exploring.	Lack of clarity	–
6-9	Startup Phase	Launch Your Biz	Wordpress, SEO, Content writing	Shiny object syndrome, Investment costs.	–
9-12	Startup Phase	Grow your mailing list	Traffic generation, handling social media effectively. Communicati on, Networking	Getting visitors, Converting them to subscribers, Being consistent in content creation.	–
12-15	Growth Phase	Earn your first dollar. Launch Your service/ Product.	Product creation, Client Acquisition, Marketing.	Task handling, Work load, learning to marketing.	₹ 5,000 – ₹ 30,000

| 15-18 | Growth Phase | Earn your first dollar. Launch Your service/ Product. | Learning Funnels, Selling Business expansion ideas, Client handling. | Client Management, Team handling. Legal terms and conditions. Handling the new work pressure. | ₹ 5,000 – ₹ 30,000 |
| 18-24 | Expansion Phase | Creating Signature Products. Building revenue systems. Automating Core tasks. | Handling automation tools, Money management, Leverage building digital tools. Paid ads. | Balancing expenses and income. Streamling the whole process. | ₹ 50,000 – ₹ 3,00,000 |

If the above image is not clear make sure to download this from the Pro Blogger's vault.

General FAQ:

Should I concentrate only on SEO to drive Organic traffic?

If you are someone heavily relying on SEO to rank your blog, pause for a minute and think. Is SEO the only thing you want to capture the audience's attention?

NO!

SEO is a part of promoting your business. It isn't everything.

Value creation should be your primary focus. Omnipotent creators dedicate themselves to their interests, consider that as their life's work and bring in valuable content.

Will it take so much time to make money blogging?

No. Everyone will take less than two years(as seen in the chart) to make money blogging. It's based on your skill set. It's dependent on How fast you adapt to new learning. Some people have earned 6 six figures in One year. It depends on your learning method and how much you invest(Time & Money). To shorten the earning period, cut down the hurdles.

What happens if I don't create a product?

You don't need to create products. Service-based businesses use blogs as their authority. You can build multiple revenue streams based on your niche, such as ads, affiliate products, and sponsorship opportunities.

Why is there no talk about Google adsense?

You can signup for Google adsense. The revenue you make from ads is meagre. You have put much effort into creating content and SEO to earn handsome money through ads.

When should I outsource my tasks?

Once you start earning a consistent income, you can outsource your tasks.

Do I need to spend on tools before earning?

Consider blogging as a business. Every business needs investment so is blogging.

Investment = Knowledge +Time+ Money

Action Steps:

1. Download "Pro bloggers vault" from link.
2. Analyse your strengths and weakness to find your call.
3. Take some time exploring the existing blogs in your favourite topic.
4. Make a list of Blogs in your topic(Your Identified skill).

CHAPTER 2

YOUR LUCRATIVE NICHE

*T*here are over <u>1.5 billion websites today.</u> [7]

Google processes over 40,000 <u>search queries every second.</u>[8]

The number of bloggers in the <u>US is expected to grow to 31.7 Million.</u>[9]

When skimming through these data, the natural question that comes to me is, " Does the world needs another blog?" My initial reaction is NO. After going through many iterations and thinking from different angles, I reframed the question.

"Does the world needs another Netflix show?"

Netflix has produced over <u>1,500 original titles</u>[10] since it began producing original content in 2013. Even after watching millions of shows, why do we watch new movies and run to the theatre?

We want new movies and new shows that entertain us in various ways. We don't hate the old ones. We still watch them, but we need fresh perspective content. Agreed?

What does that say about starting a blog?

The world no more needs the same blog. The world needs a blog that is,

- New and relevant (Innovative concept)
- Old and Updated to the current scenario

Let me share an easy example to interpret the above idea. At first, the world doesn't need another food blog or parenting blog. As there are 50,000 active blogs today.[11]

We evolve every day with new inventions and strategies. This world is moving too fast towards meta-development. Most agree that we don't need a social media app, either.

Remember the story of TikTok? After purchasing musical.ly in 2017, TikTok adopted and reinvented the wheel of social media. They offered a better user experience giving access to short-form videos and collaborations with others. So how did TikTok fight with its giant competitors' Facebook and youtube? Even though social media space is so crowded, TikTok outranked its competition[12] by solving real-time problems better. Here the problem is nothing but people need a different

Similarly, despite the competitive food, parenting, and travel blogs, you can still launch a blog in these spaces and be successful.

I know you might have heard these things before,

- Stay away from niches that are too competitive
- Your Niche has to be original
- Niche down to find your audience
- Refrain from tempting an unknown niche.

Just throw all these statements from your mind.

Suppose there are several blogs on a topic(which means too competitive). In that case, that assures a validation of the existing audience for your blog. There is a demand for the information, products and services related to that Niche.

Those big blogs with a 250K+ audience might chunk your blog initially, but not everyone will resonate with how you write. This is how new blogs survive.

Is it too late to start a blog?

The Internet has allowed us to put a message in front of 4.5 billion people through the digital medium. The Digital medium is Writing, speaking, design and video through various platforms. Some choose writing as their creative outlet. Some create videos, and that's their way of sharing their ideas. When Facebook evolved, most people were talking about the death of blogging. I have been blogging for almost 6 years, and every year, I see content with the title(Clickbait title) "Is blogging dead in 2022? ".

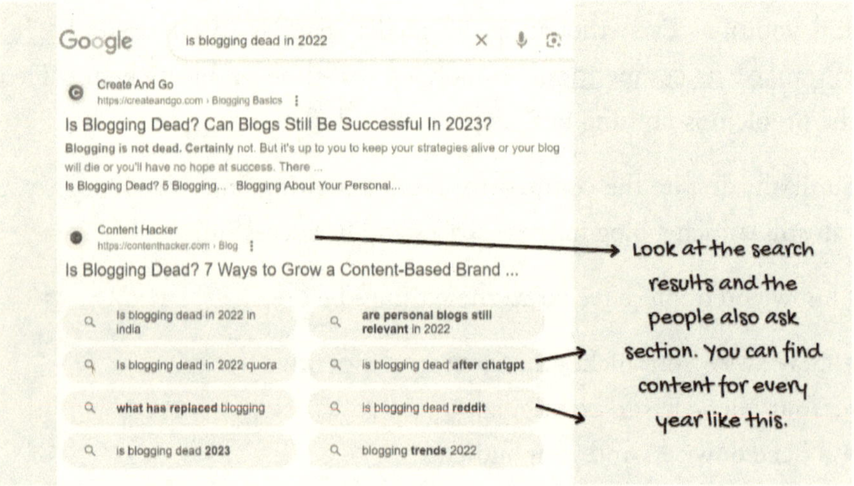

Once the TikTok search results took off on the first page of Google, people were still talking about the death of blogging. Nothing has changed in blogging for almost 20 years now. Blogging is evolving every day, tearing off unwanted things every year.

Look at the answers from quora for the above question. [13]

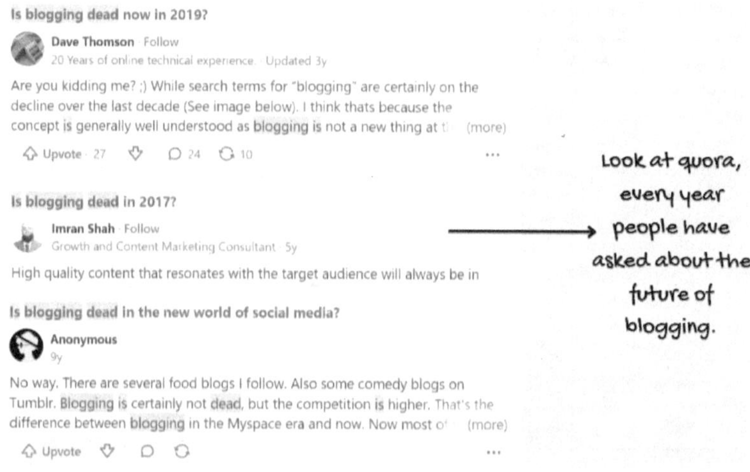

Let's look at India's blogosphere modelled by the idea diffusion curve. Amit Agarwal started **Labnol.org**[14] in 2004, and only a few bloggers were there then. He was the early adopter of the new technology. Later, you can see the emergence of innovators like Shradha Sharma- **Your story.com**[15] and Harsh Agarwal - **Shoutmeloud.com**[16]. Even if you are not an early adopter, you can still be an innovator or in an early majority in 2023. After this pandemic, there has been **a sheer rise in the volume of bloggers**[17] in India. This is because the idea of making money through the blog has been diffused well among the Indians.

So, there is always time to start a blog. All you wanted to ask yourself is

- **Where can I be an Innovator?** Look at the example of **Yourstory. com** - When people were adopting blogging, she wanted to share the stories of small startups. Now Yourstory.com is the most prominent media platform for startups in India. While working as a journalist for the CNBC news channel and the Times of India, she realised it's easy to write about successful people. That realisation led to the start of yourstory.com, where she talks about less celebrated people with dreams and a sense of purpose.

IDEA-DIFFUSION CURVE

	INNOVATORS	EARLY ADOPTERS	EARLY MAJORITY	LATE MAJORITY	LAGGARDS
No.of Bloggers	↓	↑	↑	Beginning of Saturation. Which means there will be too many bloggers.	Over saturation
Monetising options	↓	↓	↑		
Type of blogs worked well	Broad Niche blogs, Lifestyle blogs worked well	Broad Niche blogs, Development of new monetising options	Narrow Niche blogs and sub niches worked well.	Micro niche blogs works well	

Durgathiyagarajan.in

Idea-Diffusion curve explaining the number of bloggers in each stage of the curve.

- **How can I diffuse an existing idea?** There are so many food blogs, as you know. **Mylittlemoppet.com**[18] diffused the concept of food blogging with the new notion of nutritious recipes exclusive to toddlers and kids.

People Create content for various reasons. If someone's Ikigai is personal development, they write about personal growth and lifestyle to help others have a better life. This holds true for food blogs, art blogs etc. Someone knew how to make good food and wanted to share it with the world.

In short, People create digital content to express their thoughts and ideas. Not every content is accurate, so many ranges must be distilled. This is why the content we find is 80% mediocre, and people always look for quality content.

"Even though there is a sea of content, you can still ship your quality content."

I hope the above argument satisfies your two fundamental questions,

1. Does the world need another blog?
2. Is it too late to start a blog?

If that holds well. Now it's time to start finding your Niche. Before we discuss the five-level Niche identification system, I must clarify two questions,

1. What is a Niche?
2. The Niche Archetypes and how most niches fit into that.

Everyone knows it's essential to find your Niche before starting a blog. *Niche is the topic around which you will be creating content.* This may be parenting, food, health, wealth, personal growth etc.

From Maslow's theory of Hierarchy, you can understand that people are always looking for a better solution to their problems. They are always looking for betterment. This doesn't need to be money. It could fall under any one category below

- Health
- Wealth
- Fashion
- Travel
- Food
- Budgeting
- Personal Finance
- Retirement, and so on.

Think of your topic/Niche as the problem it solves. Every Niche begins with you/Your skill. Your talent for understanding and expressing your opinions. Your skill must fit in the market so that you can build an ever-lasting business out of your blog.

If you have created your learning ladder from chapter 1, you have done half of the work. Let's find a path to fit your skill in the market.

Niche Archetypes:

Blogs can be segregated into two main categories.

1. General Blogs (News, Expressing thoughts, DIY etc.)
2. Community-Based blogs (Problem-solving blogs etc.)

General blogs:

Blogs that talk about general information like News, hacks and tips on people's overall well-being come under this category.

NICHE ARCHETYPES

General / Resource Blogs

Strengths	Weaknesses
• Highest Earning potential • You need to concentrate only on this. • Targets general audience. • Drive traffic more easily	• Compete with big media companies • You need to do more initial work • Your topic should be broader to receive more links.

Ex: Tech tutorial blogs, News sites, Authority sites on Niches etc

Consider Fonearena.com started in 2008 that reviews every mobile phone. Homes247.in talks about real estate in India. Stylecraze.com shares various topics under fashion. Caravan.com talks politics and News. Similarly, you have many big media companies like the Times of India, Mint and blogs that talk about celebrities, Hollywood, Bollywood etc. It caters for a wide range of audiences. Starting general blogs fits in if you are an Introvert with great ideas and thoughts. You need not be the centre of attraction. Your words speak for you.

Community-Based Blogs:

These blogs serve a unique group of people.

Community-based blogs are either problem-solving or Product based. Think of your Niche in terms of a problem it solves. One such person is Dr Hema Priya from My little moppet blog. Most working and new moms struggled to provide nutritious food to their babies. She started recipes for toddlers and kids. You can find month-appropriate recipes for babies eliminating the trouble moms face when feeding the same food. This is how her blog differentiated from the other food blogs; soon after she got good reviews for her recipes, she started selling packed foods for babies. That is how she converted her blog into a business.

NICHE ARCHETYPES

Community Blogs

strengths	weaknesses
• You can develop yourself • You are the hero, the community runs based on your value- Personal brand.	• You need to create content. • You cannot outsource every type of content • Money making option is less, compared to other blog models. • You need to develop your own products to make more income.

Today Little moppets have few physical outlets too.

As discussed in chapter 1, if you have chosen a development-based path, this community-based blog fits in. You learnt a skill and want to teach it to others and build a community around it. Personal brands come under community blogs. Suppose you're going to start an amazon affiliate site and Niche it to a particular audience. In that case, that's a community blog.

Finding Your Sweet Spot:

You have now understood how to turn your skill into a business. The most important differentiator from the existing blogs is

1. What problem do you find in your Niche?
2. What Innovative idea do you have for the problem?
3. How do you share those ideas?
4. What Product fits the market?

Let's do that practically for someone who wants to start a Blog. Here are the steps you need to follow. You can do this deep research with the help of the workbook included in this book.

1. Find your skill (Using the SWOT test in chapter 1) or write if you know what you are skilled in.
2. Do a detailed study about that topic. Make a list of blogs that rank on the first 3 pages.
3. When researching, distil the information by segregating the blogs based.
   a) The type of content they produce
   b) What problems do they solve?
   c) What are the Products they are selling? Or their general monetisation method
   d) Who is their audience?
4. You have sorted out everything; now it's your time to choose whether you are going to
   a) Innovate or inject new ideas or
   b) Give a better solution(Using products like courses, e-books etc.)for an existing problem.

5. There might be media sites or early adopters who have been blogging about photography for 10+ years. You cannot directly compete with them, as they have already been authorised by Google. You can narrow down your interest to a particular topic. Not just photography but photography for food bloggers or For Modelling women.

6. Once you have narrowed down your idea, restart the process with your case. Google "Photography for Food bloggers." Do deep research with the steps mentioned earlier.

7. If you need help finding problems in your Niche, **you can use this tool to find the subreddits.**[19] That way, you can find more narrowed-down topics. When surfing through subreddits you can find the problems in your niche.

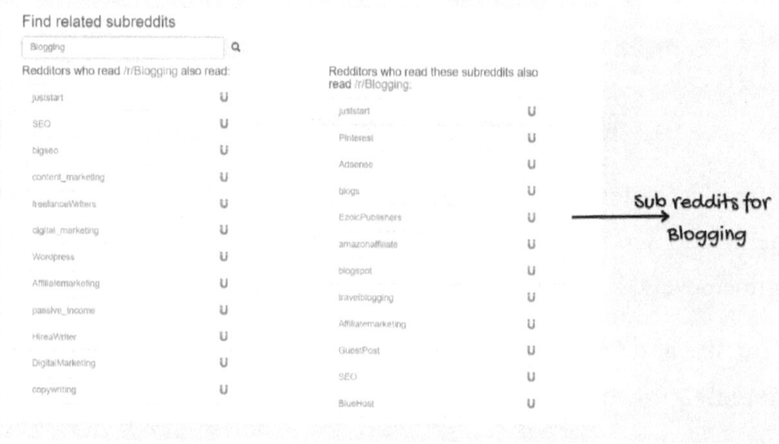

If you have identified some topics, that's great. The basics of a great Niche is fourfold.

1. Your skill should match the market.
2. Presence of an existing audience.
3. Your target audience's pain points.
4. Ability to create products/services.

If you still need help choosing the Niche, look at the table below- 6 Profitable Niches and Sub niches. These are not just the Profitable Niches.

I just curated them based on the number of bloggers and the ease of creating content. You can pick them as an example and reiterate them for yours.

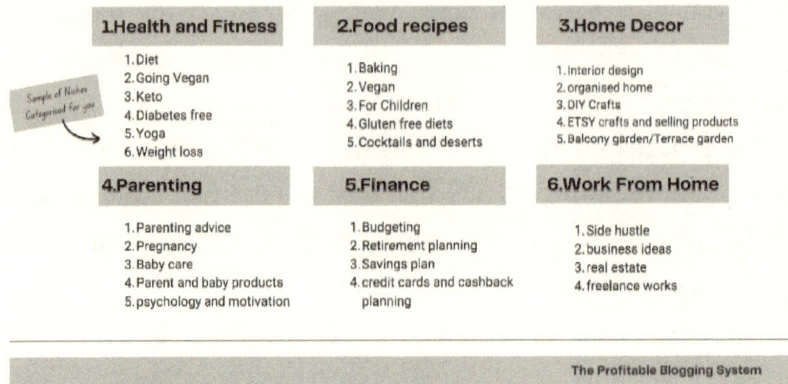

Matching the Market Potential:

The market potential of a blog refers to the potential demand for the content and services offered and the potential for the blog to generate revenue.Several factors can affect the market potential of a blog, including:

1. The size and growth potential of the market: The more enormous and rapidly growing the market is, the more potential it is for a blog to succeed.

2. Competition: If there is a lot of competition in a particular niche, it may be more difficult for a new blog to stand out and attract an audience.

3. The target audience: The target audience's size and characteristics can affect a blog's market potential. For example, suppose the target audience is small or has limited purchasing power. In that case, it may be more difficult for the blog to generate revenue.

4. The quality and relevance of the content: Suppose the content is high quality and addresses the needs and interests of the target audience. In that case, it is more

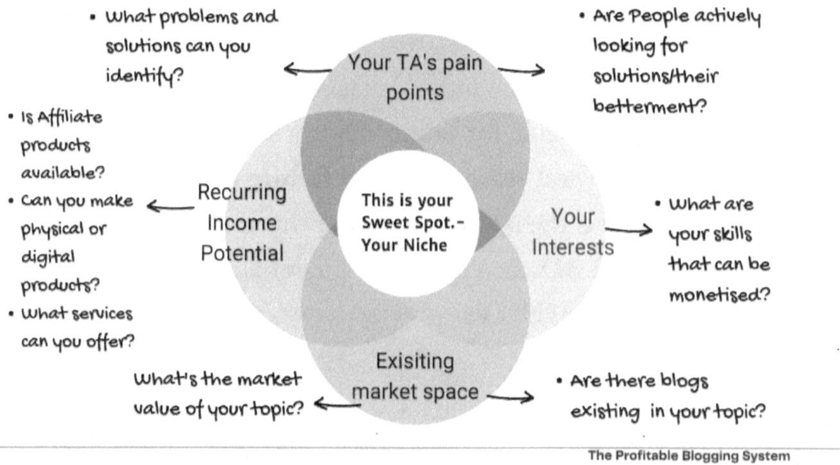

likely to attract and retain a loyal audience.

By carefully researching and evaluating these and other factors, you can better understand the market potential of a particular blog and whether it is a good fit for your business goals. It is essential when choosing a niche because it can help you determine the feasibility and profitability of your business idea. By assessing a market's size and growth potential, you can better understand whether there is demand for your product or service and whether there is room for your business to succeed.

The only reason behind blogs' failure is not identifying their market potential. Some people choose a niche that is too broad and takes a lot of time to monetise. Suppose the Niche is too narrow or untapped; in that case, the keyword difficulty might be low, so selling your products will be too difficult. There will be no space for the new audience.

Too broad and Too Narrow, is that a good to proceed?

Consider the failure of 3D TVs by big TV manufacturers like Sony, LG and Panasonic. Even though 3D movie viewing goes back decades, the release of *Avatar* in 2009 was an ultimate game-changer. With its worldwide 3D success, movie studios not only started pumping out a steady stream of 3D movies into movie theatres but TV makers, beginning with Panasonic and LG, made 3D available for home viewing with the introduction of 3D TV. **There are several reasons for the failure of 3D TVs.**[20] But the most prominent one is the lack of buyers for the TV. Not everyone liked viewing everything in 3D. So the market potential was significantly less, leading to the failure of 3D TVs.

What this has to say with choosing the Niche?

1. A too-broad topic like Parenting - Takes too much time, effort and money to build a sustainable blog.
2. Too Narrow topics like Luxury products for pets- It is too hard to monetise as the audience is minimal.
3. Finding the topic that has evergreen potential is how you grow smoothly.

Consider this blog **Tinyhouseblog.com**. The whole blog is about tiny houses serving a minimal audience and thriving. Likewise, if your products have good potential, you can even serve a minimal audience. A good equilibrium for a niche is to have an optimal audience with good market value.

Finding the Market Value of a Niche:

Understanding the online market ecosystem helps you take a great decision. The ecosystem consists of you, your competitor, the big sharks, media sites,influencers,curators and small businesses serving your Niche. Everyone here creates content for their needs. You have to clearly differentiate your competitor from others. Sometimes collaboration works very well than the competition. Small businesses in your industry create products that lead you to make money through affiliate marketing. They are your link creators. Look at the picture below, which shares how your audience is shared by your ecosystem.

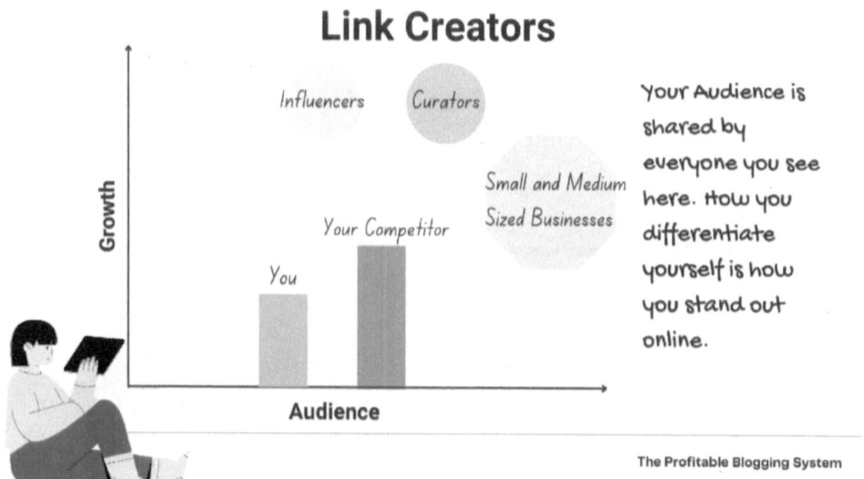

Each and every one is important for your growth. These people, have laid the initial steps. for you Now it's your turn to find the potential gap or reiterate the wheel.

I hope you understand the theory behind choosing the Niche. Let's estimate the market value of a Niche practically. To do this, you can use the **Niche Identification workbook and Spreadsheet**. Here I am outlining the whole process so that it will be easy for you to carry on with your topic. If you have chosen your Niche following the steps mentioned above in chapters 1 and 2, this market research is easy.

We will analyse the market value by exploring the website marketplaces, content marketplaces, available affiliate products and ability to create products.

I am going to do this exercise for the Niche - Content Writing.

Step 1:Analysing the website marketplaces:

When you go through the website marketplaces where people sell their blogs, you can find the selling worth of that topic. (Not everyone will sell, but the value says how well the demand is). I choose **Flippa.com** and **Empireflippers.com** to check the potential for the Niche. Navigate to Flippa.com and enter your Niche. Check the selling price of the blog below, which says that there is good demand and the profit margin of the existing creator is good. So, there is great potential to go ahead with this Niche.Check on empire flippers too.

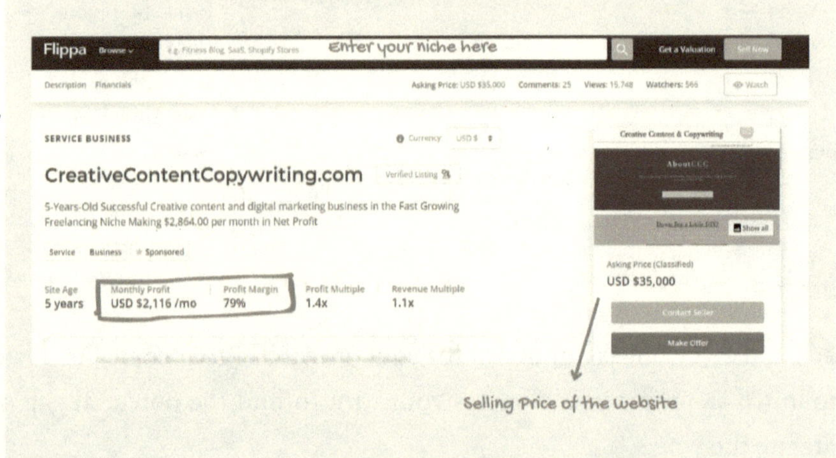

Step 2: Analysing the Content Marketplaces:

Content marketplaces are where people sell their courses, digital products etc. The Popular content marketplaces you can use - are Udemy, Etsy etc. Do a general google search

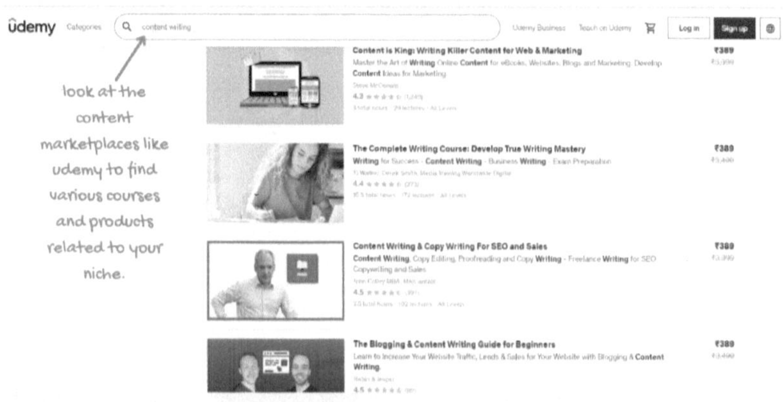

Step 3: Finding the Affiliate Products.

The above steps 1 and 2 help you find market value and product creation ideas for your Niche. While doing the research, you can find big sharks and competitors in your place. It's time to find the affiliate products in your Niche. You can make money by promoting good products and sponsored posts. It is a simple process, either. You can check on the affiliate network sites or use google search operators. There are several ways to find affiliate products in a specific niche:

1. Research affiliate networks: Many companies offer affiliate programs and list their products on affiliate networks. Some popular affiliate networks include Commission Junction, Amazon Associates, and ClickBank. You can search these networks for products in your Niche.

2. Check out popular e-commerce websites: Websites like Amazon and eBay have a wide variety of products in many different niches. You can browse these websites and look for products that might be suitable for your audience.

3. Use keyword research tools: You can use keyword research tools like Google Keyword Planner or Ahrefs to find popular keywords in your Niche. These tools can help you identify relevant products and brands for your audience.

4. Look for blog posts or articles about products in your Niche: Many bloggers and content creators review and recommend products in their Niche. You can search for blog posts or articles related to your Niche to find products that suit your audience.

5. Reach out to companies directly: If you can't find a product you're interested in promoting through any of the above methods, you can reach out to companies instantly to see if they have an affiliate program. Many companies will be happy to work with affiliates, especially if you have a large following or a well-established website in your Niche.

Using search operators to find Affiliate products:

Here are a few Google search operators you can use to find affiliate products in a specific niche:

1. *"affiliate program" + keyword:* This will search for websites with an affiliate program and include the keyword in their website or product description. For example, "affiliate program" + "fitness equipment" will return websites with an affiliate program for fitness equipment.

2. *"become an affiliate" + keyword:* This will search for websites that have a page or section on their website where you can sign up to become an affiliate. For example, "become an affiliate" + "pet supplies" will return websites with a page for signing up to become an affiliate for pet supplies.

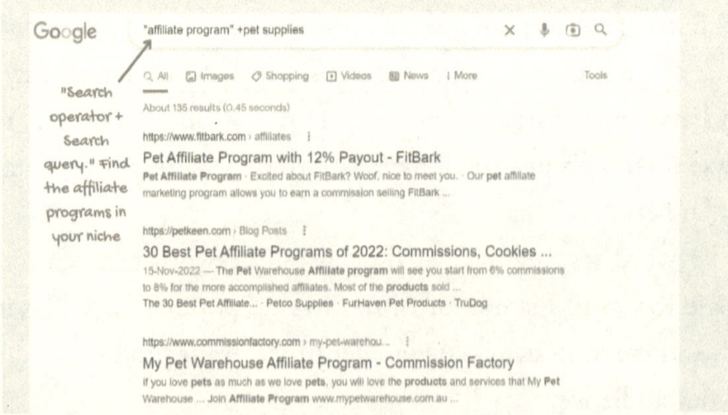

3. ***"affiliate marketing" + keyword:*** This will search for websites and resources that discuss affiliate marketing and include the keyword in their content. For example, "affiliate marketing" + "beauty products" will return websites and resources that discuss affiliate marketing for beauty products.

4. ***"recommended products" + keyword:*** This will search for websites and resources that recommend products in a specific niche. For example, "recommended products" + "outdoor gear" will return websites and resources that recommend outdoor gear products.

Remember that these search operators may only return results for some Niche. Still, they can be a good starting point for finding affiliate products in your area of interest.

Now that you have a whole list of ideas, well prepared for a blogging startup. If you have done everything step by step, as mentioned in the workbook, even if you have so many skills, you can figure out which works best.

Overcome fears about picking the Niche:

Picking a niche can be intimidating because it involves committing to a specific area of focus and potentially limiting your audience. I get emails from my readers stating

- I am not an expert in any area
- What If I have chosen the wrong Niche?
- As you say, I have too many interests and find it hard to stick to one.

Fear 1: I am not an expert in any area:

To state frankly, no one is born an expert.

Experts are made. Experts are made from the inside out. You have the potential inbuilt within you. God has provided the quality by birth; all you need to do is stimulate your potential, overcome your barriers, and succeed.

For instance, consider a child studying 4th grade. Do you tell him as an expert?

No.

But in the perception of a 2nd-grade child, a 4th-grade child is an expert.

Do you agree with me?

This is the same rule that applies here. There are people out there still searching for an opportunity to earn. All you can do is start with what you know and keep yourself upgraded as your blog grows.

Fear 2: What if I have chosen the wrong Niche?

This happens the most time. It happened even to me. At first, I was blogging about my Engineering subjects. I was running a blog that helped many Engineering students. I created an online course for a competitive exam. It was so good to go. But my interest towards marketing has outgrown Engineering, and I started writing about digital marketing and Blogging.

Symptoms of Choosing the Wrong Niche:

1. You run out of ideas so quickly.
2. You are not interested in writing articles.
3. You can't find other bloggers in your Niche. (My Niche was too narrow, and I couldn't find other bloggers in my Niche)
4. You don't have any other affiliate options other than your products(I faced this issue)

These signs all show that you need to tweak your Niche. Many successful bloggers shifted their focus when they realised what they were doing wasn't working anymore.

Overall, the key is to take your time and not rush into a decision. Do your research, test the waters, and seek guidance if you need it. By following the above steps, you can overcome your fears and make a confident decision about your Niche.

Fear 3: I have too many interests.

My best advice for this question would be,First, choose a niche and grow your audience and earn, then introduce your audience to your other Niche that interests you. This will end successfully.

Now that you have learnt all things about choosing a Niche. It's the very important step before leaning in. I suggest you choose a Niche before going ahead with this book. Everything in the next chapters will be useful once you have chosen a Niche along with your Market ecosystem. Yes it's essential to make note of Big sharks in your Niche, The small businesses and Influencers so that you can collaborate with them later on.

Action Steps:

1. Download the Niche Research Workbook and Spreadsheet.
2. Make list of Top 5 bloggers, Small businesses, Affiliate programs, Courses, Products in your Niche.
3. Understand how others are monetising. Make a Note of it in the Spreadsheet.

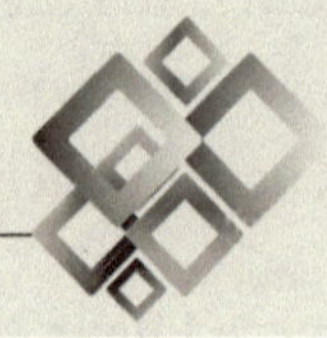

CHAPTER 3

FINDING YOUR CREATIVE EDGE

*W*riting online can change your life. Great articles let you open unexpected doors like new jobs or professional advancement.

Michael Hyatt says, ***"Writing online allows you to reach a global audience and connect with people from all walks of life."*** Expressing your thoughts and ideas to thousands is a challenging task. The best decision I have ever made is to become a blogger; it's also incredibly hard. It is about more than just the amount of work you put in; your credibility is at risk for some reasons.

A blogger's credibility may be at risk if they publish content perceived as inappropriate, expose their personal information, lead to legal issues, or have negative professional consequences. It is essential for bloggers to be aware of these risks and to take steps to protect their capital.

It's best to draw a line of trust (*a digital contract*) with your audience initially. It becomes hard to scale later if you don't set expectations at the start. This unwritten digital contract with your audience builds credibility and trust, making you feel regret-free.

It's okay to start a blog to make money, to sell your products, to share your words and write about your travel experience or promote and market things that make you money. But your blog has to attract people for you to do any of that.

Your content is the hub that brings people to your blog. Your content has to educate, entertain, inspire, teach or help your readers in some way. So it's essential to define your blog purpose. It is the first step to positioning yourself among the mass, Next is to identifying your one reader and the final one is making the digital contract.

Niche Positioning

Niche positioning refers to a specific focus or specialization within a larger market or industry. It involves identifying a target audience or customer base and tailoring products or services to meet their unique needs and preferences.

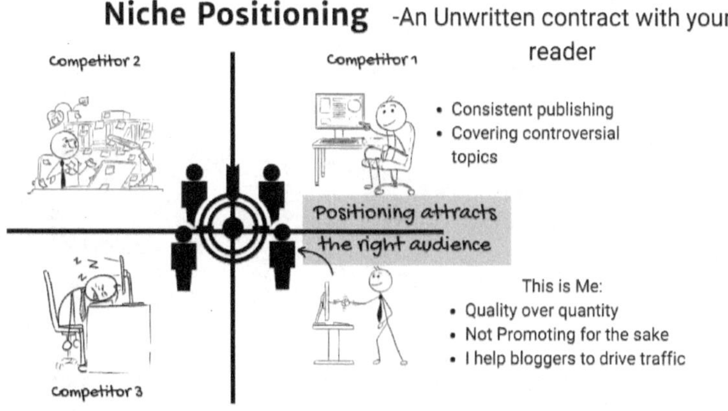

For example, a company that sells outdoor gear may have a niche positioning as a provider of high-quality, eco-friendly products for hikers and backpackers. This niche positioning sets the company apart from other outdoor gear companies and allows it to target a specific market segment.

Niche positioning can benefit businesses because it allows them to differentiate themselves from their competitors and target a specific group of customers. It can also help companies to build a strong brand identity and establish themselves as experts in their field. You can understand the importance of positioning in your Niche with a few more examples.

1. A natural skincare brand that positions itself as the go-to choice for consumers looking for clean, non-toxic, and eco-friendly products. Ex: Kama Ayurveda and Forest Essentials. Both brands serve people who want ayurvedic beauty products. But they differentiate themselves very clearly by defining their edge cleverly. While Kama ayurveda focuses on Being kind to skin and people working on their firm, Forest essentials focus on luxurious ayurvedic products. Product costs differ for both brands; they are very well-reputed brands in India.

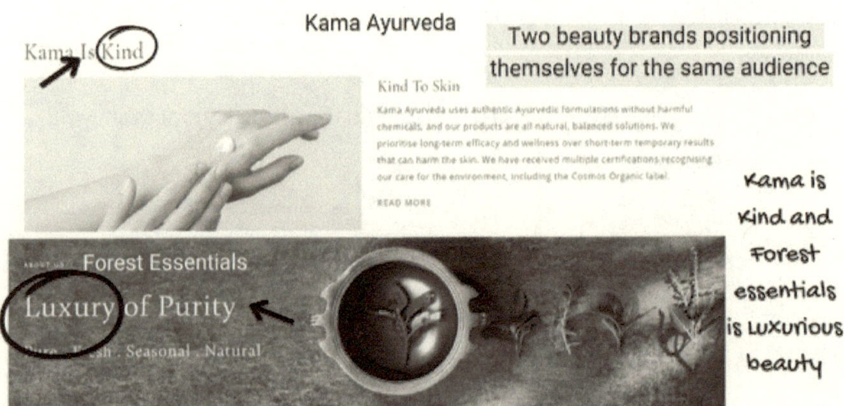

2. A luxury watch brand that positions itself as the premier choice for collectors and enthusiasts, offering high-end, hand-crafted timepieces with intricate detailing and rare materials.

3. A boutique fitness studio that positions itself as the premier choice for individuals looking for personalized, high-intensity workouts in a supportive and inclusive environment.

4. A vegan bakery that positions itself as the go-to choice for plant-based desserts and treats, offering a wide range of vegan-friendly options for special occasions or everyday indulgences.– satvicmovement.org

5. A handmade jewellery brand that positions itself as the premier choice for unique, artisanal pieces, using rare and unusual materials and offering one-of-a-kind designs.

These examples illustrate how companies can use niche positioning to differentiate themselves from their competitors and target specific market segments with specialized products and services.

With the above-stated examples, you should be able to convey your blog's message in a single sentence. It is often followed by brands and products but rarely done with content.

How can you come up with a value proposition for your blog? You start by defining your circumference and drilling into them to get specific, just like digging the well.

For instance, My main business is teaching people to write content. But not just any type of content writer- a Ghostwriter.

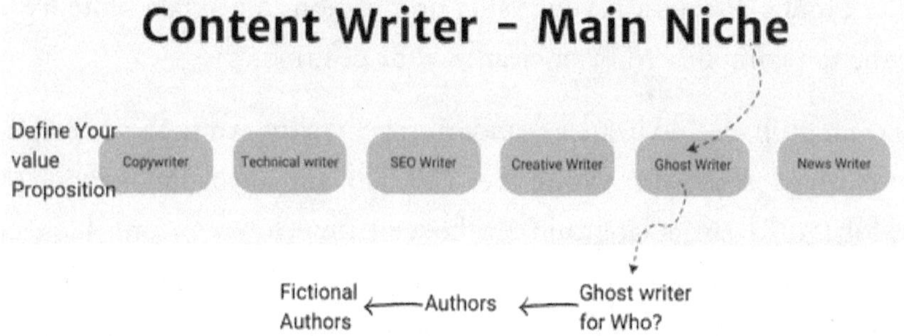

A ghostwriter for Authors(Who). Not just any kind of author. Ghostwriting for Fictional authors.

Once you break it down this way, your content takes on a particular dimension.

Now I positioned myself in my Niche as a Ghostwriter for Fictional Authors.

Writing Your Creative Edge

Once you have positioned yourself, you must create a single-liner for your blog. It should touch on these two things:

1. The most significant pain point you are solving.
2. Distinguishing you from your closest competitor.

Here are some examples,

1. "The ultimate social media management platform" - **Hootsuite**
2. "The world's leading CRM" - **Salesforce**
3. "The all-in-one marketing platform" - **HubSpot**
4. "The easiest way to create and share visual content" - **Canva**
5. "The world's leading web analytics solution" - **Google Analytics**
6. "The world's leading email marketing platform" - **Mailchimp**
7. "The ultimate SEO platform" - **Ahrefs**
8. "The ultimate lead generation tool" - **Leadpages**

If you cannot distinguish your value proposition in a single sentence, it may be too complicated or unclear in your position.

A meaningful specific beats a wandering generality. An inch wide and a mile deep. Most people earning over $50,000 annually from blogging say they focus on a particular group. At the same time, lower-income bloggers are evenly split between focusing on a narrow audience or a broad one. **Growthbadger study on bloggers**[21] has revealed this major takeaway.

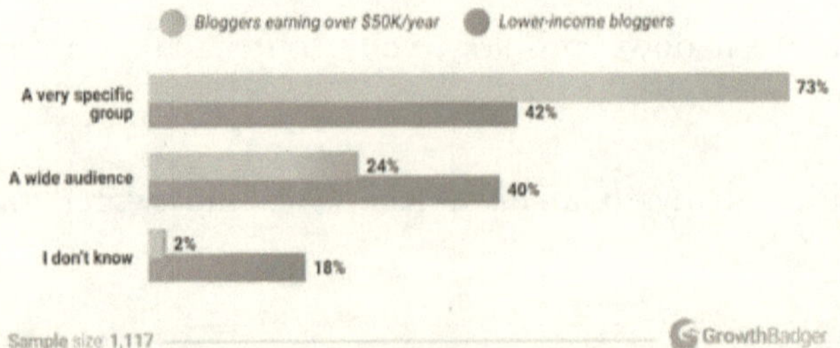

- **73%** of bloggers who earn over $50,000 per year typically publish content focused on the interests of very specific groups, compared to only **42%** of lower-income bloggers who do the same.
- Compared to higher-income bloggers, lower-income bloggers are nine times as likely not to know whether their content is more interesting to a wide audience or a narrow one.

Here are a few more examples from top bloggers:

1. "Helping busy moms make time for themselves" - The Mom Crowd.
2. "Empowering creatives to turn their passions into a business" - The Merriweather Council.
3. "Helping you live your best life on a budget" - The Frugal Girl.
4. "Inspiring a love of reading, one book at a time" - Reading with Robin.
5. "Making the most of your money and your life" - The Simple Dollar.
6. "Helping you build a better future through personal finance" - Financial Samurai.
7. "Empowering women to create the life and business of their dreams" - She Takes on the World.
8. "Helping you achieve your health and fitness goals" - Fit Foodie Finds
9. "Inspiring you to live your best life, one adventure at a time" - Pinch of Yum.
10. "Helping you turn your passion into a successful business" - The Middle Finger Project.

Once you have identified your one-liners like this, make sure you use them in your blog's main header like this one from **She corporated**.[22]

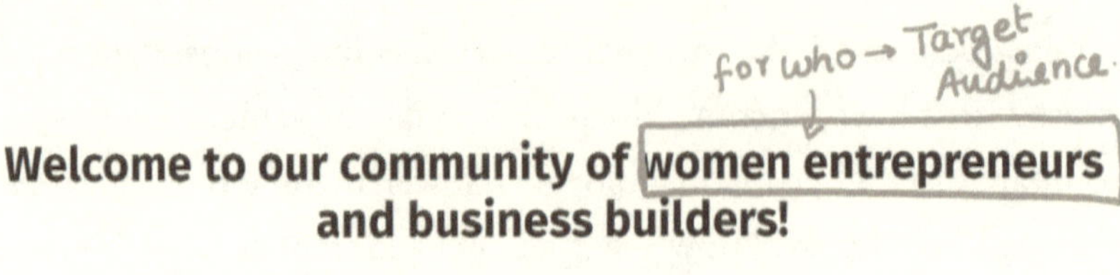

Plug and Play template for your one-liner:

1. **"Helping [customer group] achieve [desired outcome] through [unique value proposition]."**
Example: "Helping busy professionals achieve work-life balance through on-demand virtual fitness classes."

2. **"Making [task or process] easier/better/more enjoyable for [customer group] through [unique value proposition]."**
Example: "Making home cleaning easier and more enjoyable for busy families through eco-friendly products and convenient scheduling options."

3. **"Elevating [customer experience] with [unique value proposition]."**
Example: "Elevating the dining experience with gourmet, farm-to-table cuisine and exceptional service."

4. **"Transforming [problem or challenge] into [positive outcome] with [unique value proposition]."**
Example: "Transforming financial stress into financial stability with personalized financial planning and investment strategies."

In simple words, write.

I help/teach/inspire______________who want to ____________

Example: I teach ghostwriters who want to build publishing company.

Remember to use this one-liner in your Blog's header, social profiles etc.

Your One Reader:

"The secret to writing well for the web is to write for one person, not for a million." - Seth Godin.

A true fan is someone who benefits from your solution. When you are starting to build a blog, you must write for them first.

If you can cultivate and find 100 true fans willing to spend a certain amount on your products, you can build a sustainable business.

As J.K Rowling says, *"Writing to one person allows you to be more specific, more detailed, and more personal, which can make your writing more powerful and effective."*

When writing to many, you need to consider the interests and needs of a diverse audience and tailor your content accordingly. When writing to one, you can be more specific and personalized, as you have a particular individual or group in mind. Successful bloggers know their audiences well. **73%** of bloggers[23] who earn over $50,000 per year say they focus their content on the **interests of a very specific group.** Now its time to bring in a particular group of your audience. I know its tedious; I hated to do this initially, but once I figured out who I was writing to, the writing resonated well.

Remember our example of a Ghostwriter for Fictional Authors? It would help if you continued to make it more in-depth by answering these questions,

- What are their demographics?
- Where do they work?
- Where do they hang out online?
- What problems do they face daily?
- What do they enjoy doing?

- What do they hate?
- Who do they follow on social media?

You will be unsure to answer these right now. You might feel like, why should I care about these things? When you have a clear picture of your audience, whatever you write for them resonates so well with them that they become your fervent. Check the Call to Action of an Web design Agency for Authors- **Rocketexpansion.com** It is compelling for the authors to take up their service. Read every line on the Image below, look how deep they know about their audience(Authors).

CTA of an Author Web Design Agency

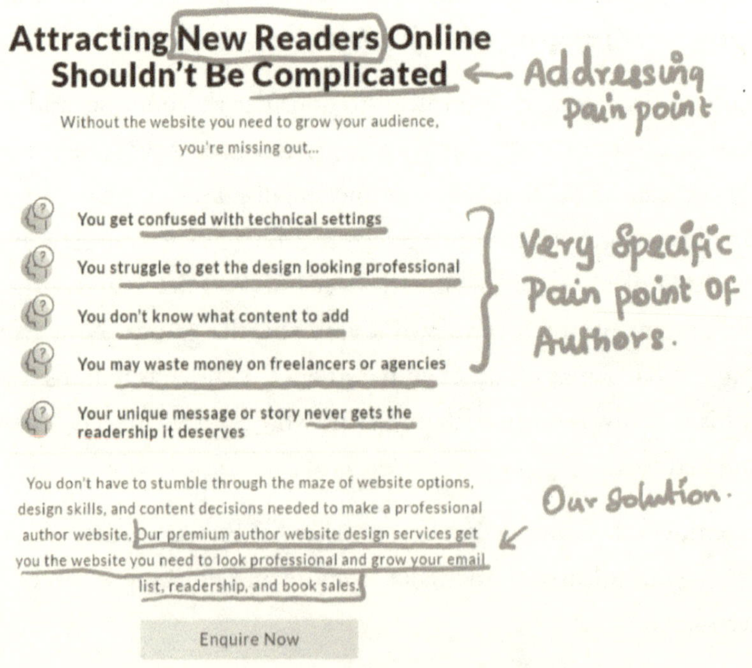

How to write my audience persona?

1. Talk to your existing audience. Ask them what they read online. How satisfying is your writing? What do they expect from you? etc

2. When you have an existing audience, you can get all the details of the above questions from your Google Analytics account.

3. Use tools like **similar web** and **sparktoro** to get more details about your competitor's audience.

4. You can check the Facebook group conversations of your reader community. If you are Writing for New moms, find a few active Facebook groups of Moms and note their discussion on their problems.

5. You can check Quora, Reddit and Niche community forums the same way.

Talking to the audience and building your community early on will save you hours and dollars later when you launch your products.

A great example of Niche positioning and audience targeting is Firstcry.com. The founder of Firstcry.com, Mr Supam Maheshwari, found that the market of baby and kids products needed to be more organized in India(During 2009 & 2010). Even though Firstcry was pitching against its giant competitors, Amazon and Flipkart, it won the market by building a loyal New Mom fan base. Firstcry understood that only some of the tier 2 &tier 3 cities in India were using the Internet to get products. So they used a hybrid model of having both online and offline stores. The very first touching point of Firstcry was they reached the hospitals to give Free Giftbox to new moms and turned new moms into micro-influencers. Now they call themselves "India's Finest Platform for Baby care products".

Amazon Vs FirstCry

	amazon.com	firstcry
Product/Audience Focus	Focuses on wide range of products catering general audience	Focuses on Baby and Mom's Products. This makes it a go-to destination for parents and caregivers looking for these types of products.
Geographic Focus	Operated Globally.	Primarily Focuses on Indian Market. This means that it has a strong presence in India and is familiar with the needs and preferences of customers in this market.
Business Model	Online	Online + Offline Stores

> **Fact #3:** FirstCry is a true testament to the fact that you can survive & thrive even in a highly competitive industry by carving out a niche for yourself.
>
> ***Action step:*** *Position your idea on your niche. It might take sometime, but you can do it !*

I shared this one here because I treat blogging as a startup; that way, when you perform everything like a startup, You can build a Profitable Business from Day 1.

I hope you understand the importance of choosing your Niche, positioning in the Niche and defining your audience. Let's build your digital home in the next chapter.

Action Steps:

1. Download Audience Persona workbook and start answering the questions.
2. Model and Analyse the top blogs in your niche.
3. Write your One-liner. Just write a rough one. You modify as you evolve.
4. Write your digital contract by mentioning what problem you solve for your who.

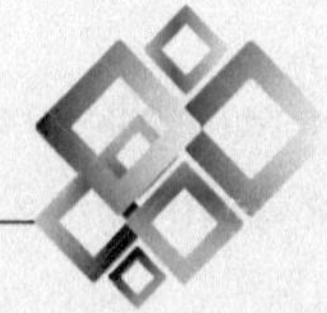

CHAPTER 4

YOUR DIGITAL TECH STACK

*I*t's time to start building your digital home. A digital home helps you establish yourself as a thought leader in your Niche, helping you develop connections, network and influence people through your content. As you build your website, you will need the following things:

1. A domain
2. A hosting
3. A blogging platform(CMS)
4. An Email Service Provider
5. Plugins - to optimize Website, SEO, Speed
6. Analytics

Across each of these areas, there are a lot of platforms out there. I am not going to cover all of them. Going in-depth and comparing the features is optional when you are just starting out. As you evolve, you will explore multiple platforms as your needs change with a growing email list and monetizing options.

The problem with most beginners is they obsess over tech tools and themes of their blogs. I have even seen people spend too much time fixing their blog's theme and tech stack. If you are at the beginning of your journey, save time and effort figuring out your tech stack by choosing a minimal one.

The reality is no one ever cares about what tech stack you are using. In most cases, No one wants to know what tech stack you are using. They are least bothered about it. Have you ever thought of what tech stack Instagram is built upon? When using Instagram, you only care whether it meets your needs. You never feel whether Instagram's tech stack is outdated.

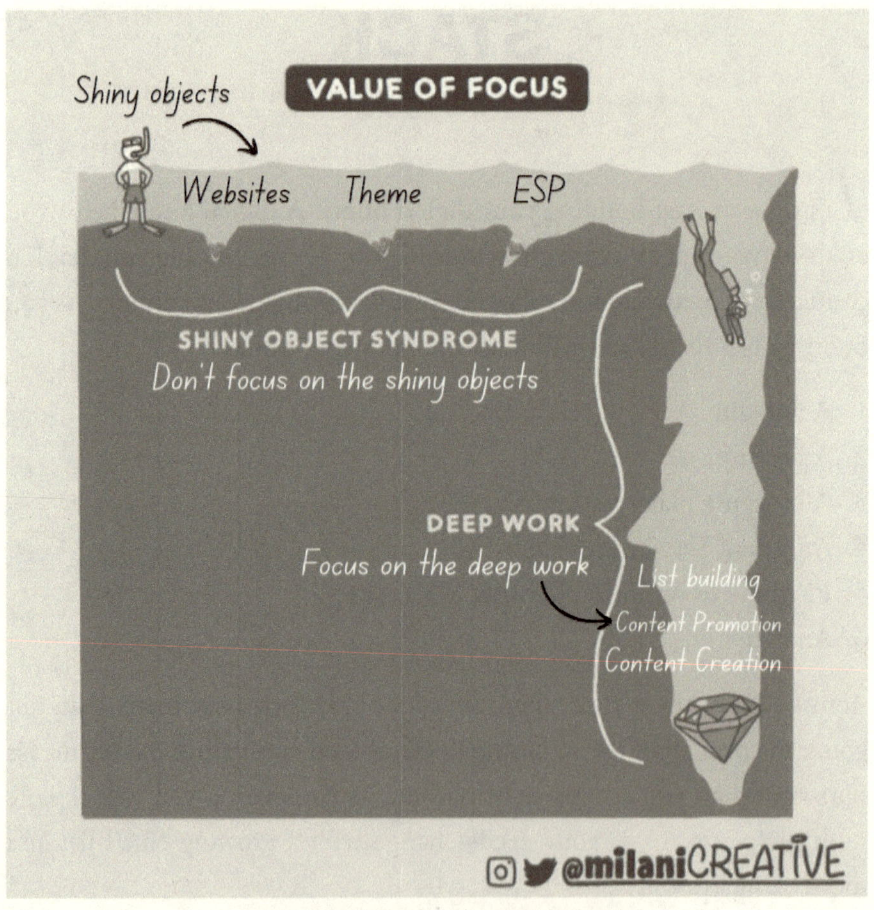

1Pic courtesy- @milaniCreative24

What's important here is finding something good enough to start. Focus more on content creation, which yields meaningful results. Instead of comparing or reviewing every platform, I will emphasize critical things you should consider and avoid.

Your Digital Tech Stack

Domain:

You can buy your domain name from <u>Namecheap</u>. I purchased five of my domains from them. The best thing is that they don't overprice when renewing every year. Don't spend too much time choosing your domain name, as you have many domain name generators and sites to help along the way.

1. **Domain name generators:** <u>Domain wheel</u>, <u>Nameboy</u>, <u>Biznamewiz</u> suggestion tool.
2. **Websites:** <u>2501+ Best Blog Names Suggestions And Ideas</u>-[25] This article from Brandboy.com shares

Fix your domain name as quickly as possible.

Hosting:

Hosting plays a more important role when you are non-techy like me. I used Go-daddy, Hostgator, Bluehost, and finally found <u>Hostinger</u> serving all my needs. Hostinger's exceptional customer service helped me fix so many technical problems. Once I lost my whole website; instead of asking me to go through an article DIY, hostinger representatives helped me retrieve my website. I didn't find any other hosting companies with such a better response to their customer at that pricing. If you're looking for a much better platform with higher pricing options -<u>Cloudways</u> works very well. When choosing a hosting, you need to know that the server must be speed optimized and easy to switch whenever you want.

Blogging Platform:

When choosing a platform, go with <u>Wordpress.org</u>(not.com) or <u>Ghost.</u> The reason is that they are both open-source platforms. Ghost and WordPress.org are both popular platforms for building websites, but you should consider some essential differences when deciding which one to use.

Ghost is a relatively new open-source platform that is specifically designed for blogging. It is known for its simplicity, ease of use, and clean design. Ghost is a good choice if you want to create a personal blog or a professional online publication(Newsletter based).

WordPress.org, on the other hand, is a more established platform used by millions of websites worldwide. It is a versatile and feature-rich platform for building any website, including blogs, e-commerce stores, business websites, and more. WordPress.org is a good choice if you need a more flexible and customizable platform for your website.

Ghost is a good choice for newsletter based publication, while WordPress. org is a good choice for building any website.

Email Service Provider:

When it comes to email service providers, you need to choose the one that fits your budget. In the beginning, you can go with <u>Mailchimp</u> or <u>Mailerlite</u>. Here are some key differences between the two platforms:

- Pricing: Mailchimp offers a free plan for small lists, while MailerLite's free plan is available for lists of up to 1,000 subscribers. Mailchimp's paid plans start at $9.99 per month, while MailerLite's paid plans start at $10 per month.
- Ease of use: Both platforms are user-friendly, but Mailchimp is generally considered easier to use, especially for beginners.

- Features: Both platforms offer a wide range of parts, but MailerLite has more advanced features, such as A/B testing, landing pages, and web push notifications.
- Integrations: Both platforms offer a range of integrations with other tools and services, but Mailchimp has a more extensive selection of integrations available.

Ultimately, the choice between Mailchimp and MailerLite will depend on your specific needs and budget. It might be helpful to sign up for free trials of both platforms and try them out to see which works best for you.

Other ESPs is <u>Convertkit</u> and <u>Getresponse</u>.

Plugins:

You need plugins when using WordPress. I suggest only seven must-need plugins.

1. <u>Rankmath</u>- For SEO(Both Free and Paid versions based on your budget)
2. <u>Wordfence</u> - For Security
3. <u>Updraftplus</u>- For Backup
4. <u>Shortpixel</u>- Image Compression
5. <u>WPRocket</u>- To increase your website speed.
6. <u>Google Site Kit</u>-For linking Google services like search console and analytics
7. <u>Antispam Bee</u>- To avoid spamming

Most of them have a free version that benefits beginners. You can switch to the pro version as you evolve. More than this, if you use the Email service provider, you might need to install their plugin—anything more than this is not required until you reach 10k readers.

Designing your website:

Choosing themes:

WordPress websites require a premium theme. Premium themes are typical of a higher quality than free themes. They are usually well-designed and well-coded, which can significantly impact your website's look and performance. It often comes with more features and customization options than free themes.

I suggest only a few themes with a theme builder. Suppose you are okay with customizing without a theme builder. That's fine. For Non-techy people, theme builders are life savers.

1. Page Builder - <u>Elementor</u>
2. Premium WP themes- <u>Generatepress</u>, <u>Astra</u> and <u>Kadence.</u>

Focus on building something helpful rather than crawling inside the rat hole of perfection. When starting, you need a working system, not the best system. I had made the mistake of revamping my site most of the time, shifting from one theme to other. It all happens because you compare yourself in subzero with someone who has been blogging for about ten years. Never do that!

Your Brand Style Guide:

A brand style guide is a document that outlines the specific elements of your brand, such as your logo, colours, and font. It helps to ensure that your brand is consistently represented across all marketing materials, including your website.

Again, I only let you focus a little on these shiny objects. While doing the niche research, you might have come across so many websites. By now, you must have an idea of their colours and how the sites look.

- **To create a logo:** Go to <u>canva.com</u>, search for logo design templates, and rework for you.

- **To choose a colour palette:** You can use <u>canva's colour palette generator</u> or this <u>muzli colour palette generator.</u> Muzli colours give you an idea of how the colour palette is applied.
- **To find fonts:** You can use <u>Google fonts</u> or use simple fonts on your site.

Designing the Pages:

Your blog should have pages depending on the purpose and content of the website. Here are some standard pages that websites might include:

- **Home page**: This is the website's main page and often serves as a landing page for visitors. It typically provides an overview of the website and its content and may include links to other pages on the site.
- **About page:** This page provides information about the website and its creators or owners. It might include a history of the website, the mission or purpose of the site, and biographical information about the people behind it.
- **Contact page:** This page provides information on how visitors can get in touch with the website or its creators. It might include a contact form, an email address, and phone numbers.
- **Products or services page:** If the website is an online store or a service provider, it will likely have a page describing the products or services offered. This page might include images, descriptions, and pricing information.
- **Blog page:** The page holds the articles you write.
- **Privacy policy page:** This page explains how the website collects, uses, and protects the personal information of its visitors.

These are a few examples of the types of pages that a website/blog might have. The specific pages will depend on the needs and goals of the website. Now you need to know which blog design plan fits you.

Blog Design plan:

- Model 1 is for Content-based bloggers who are running authority sites.
- Model 2 is for Service-based bloggers who want to show their skills/ vision on the home page.

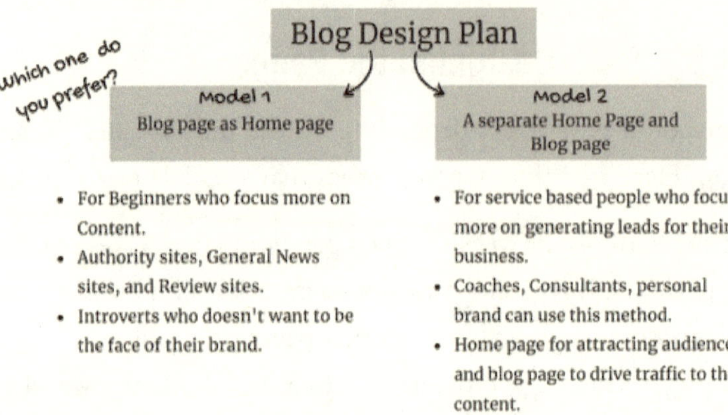

You can choose any one of the above and get started. You will have so many iterations on your websites as you grow. At this time, getting started is important.

Stylecraze is a fashion website that focuses more on content. Look at their home page below. All the articles are lined up as a Masonry brick.

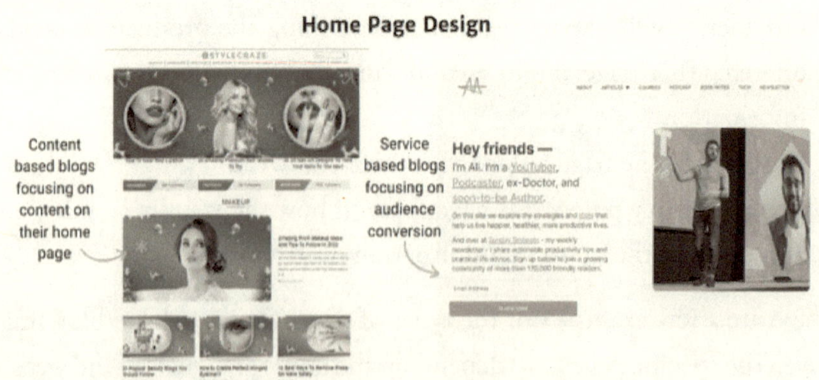

At the same time, look at Aliabdaal's blog; his home page talks about him and his products. Choose your model and start branding your site.

Designing your Home page

If you want to showcase your skills on your home page, let's understand the theory behind successful home pages and what you need to build them apart from design and colours.

Stacking your home page:

1. Navigation bar
2. Hero/Header section
3. Social Proof Indicators
4. Call to Action

Your Navigation bar should have links to the other pages. You can either have it vertically or horizontally.

The Hero section should have 1/3rd size of your page. It is often used to showcase the website's main value proposition or message and can include a combination of text, images, and calls to action. Remember the value proposition and one-liners that we created in the last chapter? You can use them in your hero section to attract your audience.

The social proof Indicators can be

- Testimonials
- Press mentions
- Awards
- Social metrics like followers and subscribers on social media.

You can add so that it builds trust with your audience.

Call to action is where you let people subscribe to your mailing list or take free consultation sessions or download your free resources. Check the screenshots shared in the last chapter.

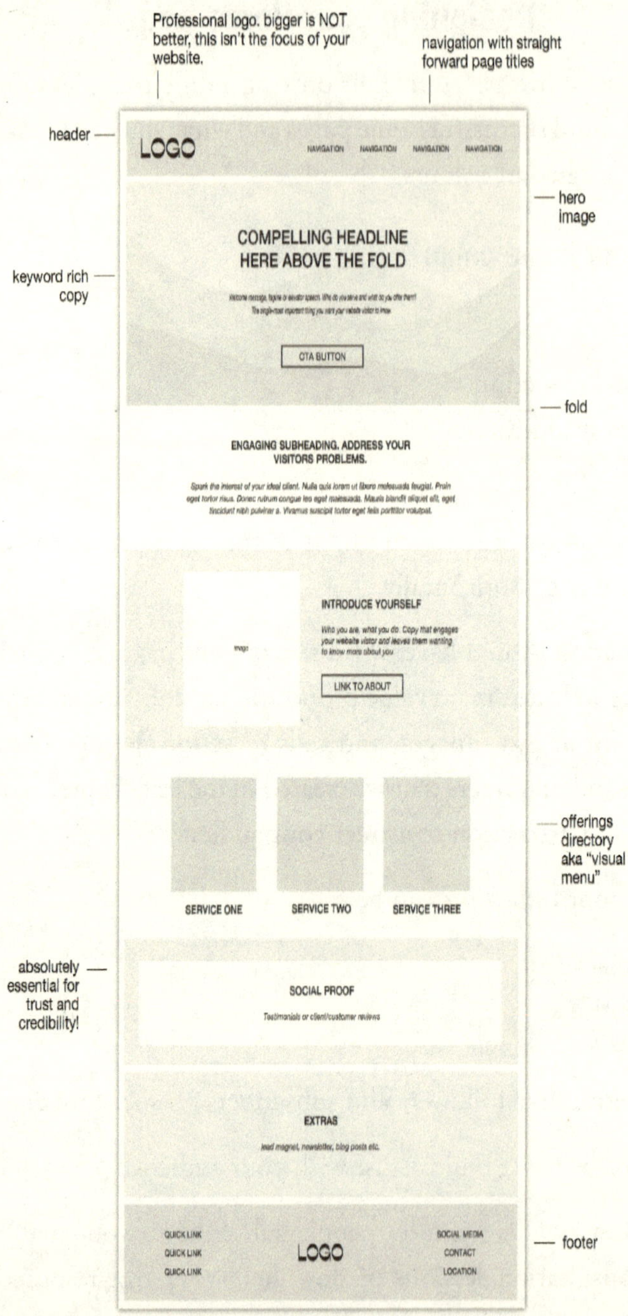

www.evermorecreativeltd.com

By now, you are ready to go ahead with pumping your content. We will focus on content creation and distribution in the following few chapters.

Action Steps:

1. Build your tech stack by choosing and purchasing the products you need.
2. Design your logo, choose colors and fonts
3. Collect inspirations and design your home page as you want.
4. Make sure you download the resources – Start a blog in 2023 and Guide to customising wordpress.
5. Design your blog the way you want. Model 1 or Model 2 Method.

PART 2

CONTENT CREATION

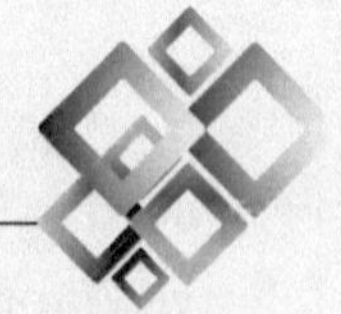

CHAPTER 5

CONTENT STRATEGY

$\mathcal{B}$uilding a solid content strategy is integral to any digital marketing plan, as it ensures that the right content is being created and distributed to the right audience at the right time.

To build your blog, you learnt the fundamentals like selecting a niche and defining your creative edge as we call your blog your digital home if you have done the action steps mentioned in the previous chapter. It would help if you defined your audience; they are the heroes to whom we direct our content.

In the following few chapters, You will learn to

1. Understand how search engines work and how we use search engines.
2. Build your content Inventory
3. Do keyword research
4. Write content & the content creation process- Wherein you will learn to create thriving SEO-optimised content.

Remember the importance of creating one-liners. Here is the one-liner of **social samosa** -Social Samosa **Enables Industry by Leading Thought and Influencing the Influencers**[26]. Check out their about page, wherein they have mentioned to whom and what they create. So social media industry is their content playing field. Similarly, Your Niche is your content playing field wherein you solve the reader's problems. Your readers want a better version of themselves; this doesn't necessarily mean making money. It could be

- Fitness
- Personal development
- Lifestyle improvement
- Finance etc

If you have made it up to this chapter, you are not a hobbyist blogger or someone who wants to make money through ads. This book is beyond that, and it helps you establish a profitable system with your audience as a centre of focus. Focusing on the better of the audience is our priority.

For Instance, Let's say I want to help people with financial literacy and the value proposition I wrote in the previous chapter is

"Transforming financial stress into financial stability with personalized financial planning and investment strategies."

From Just personalized financial planning with no audience mentioned to Just personalized financial planning for Solopreneurs.

Let's Rewrite the One-liner

"Transforming financial stress into financial stability with personalized financial planning and investment strategies for solopreneurs."

Now that you have an overview of who you will serve with your blog.

Ask yourself

1. What change your blog creates for your readers?
2. What do you want to solve?
3. How do you want them to feel after your blog posts?
4. What change your blog creates for your readers?

I imagine a friend of mine as my reader and think of the potential problems he faces financially.

Before: Spending too much to overcome corporate stress/family stress. No knowledge about handling finances or saving strategies.

After reading my blog articles, I ensure he is gaining insights on solving his problems.

After: Learn Financial planning and saving to live a well-satisfied life.

Build your content Inventory

What do you want to solve?

A list of possible things you want to solve becomes your content idea. You organize the problems into categories and create your Content Inventory. This is what people call a content calendar.

Think of your content in terms of buckets. Each category is a content bucket to achieve a particular goal or to make your customer feel a certain way.

How do you want them to feel after reading your blog posts?

Before: Overwhelmed, overspending and stressed.

After: Confident. With a better savings and investment plan.

Now you know how I went from a Niche topic to developing a blog content calendar. Look at a finance blog's extended version of the content inventory below.

sample **Content Inventory for Finance Blogs**   Monetisation: Ads + Affiliate Commission

Nick runs a personal finance blog, helping people with better saving plans by using credit cards intentionally and providing budgeting plans for safe retirement and buying a house.

Goal 1: Helping people make better use of the money they earn

Goal 2: Build/Buy a house with their earnings.

	Category 1 **Budgeting**	Category 2 **Investing**	Category 3 **Retirement**
Sub Category 1	Getting out of Debt	Buying House	Retirement planning
Sub Category 2	Small Savings Plan	Banking Plans	Rejuvenation after Retirement

The Profitable Blogging System

You can have as many content categories as you want. But I request you have a minimum of 3-5 content categories and cover in-depth articles on those categories.

Under every category, there is a subcategory you can create and write posts in those, just like the full content calendar below.

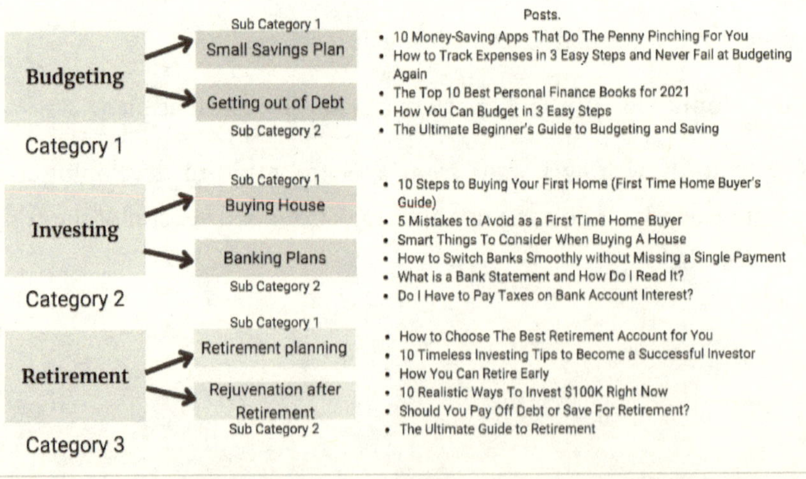

The Profitable Blogging System

If the above image overwhelms you, don't worry. In the next chapter, let's define what articles and keywords to choose for those articles.

If you are in a parenting niche, helping moms to engage with their kids meaningfully, then your categories may be

1. Activities for Toddlers - With subcategories appropriate to ages.

2. Mom Wellness

3. Toddler Food

Again, it's also based on your knowledge of those topics and heard of **Momjunction.com**?

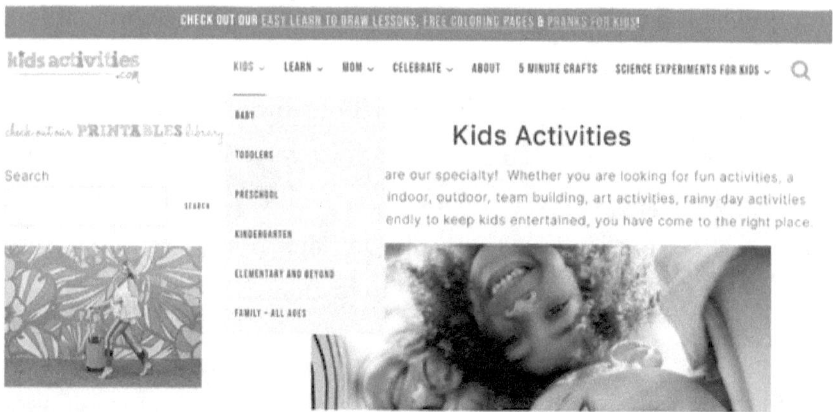

Look at the navigation bar of their home page in the image below, they are a publication with so many writers, and they have almost all the categories for Moms and kids. If you are starting, you can only cover some topics, but make sure what you cover is meaningful, just like **kidsactivitiesblog.com** and **handsonaswegrow.com**.

If you struggle to find your content buckets, you must have some issues with your value proposition. Either you are trying to cover everything, or you are confused. This content bucket is crucial as it is the skeleton of your blog.

The Site Structure

A site structure refers to how the pages on a website are organized and linked together. It typically includes the main navigation menu, sub-navigation menus and links that allow users to move between different pages on the site.

The site structure can be considered a "map" of the website, showing how the different pages and content are related. A site structure is vital for a few reasons:

1. It helps search engines understand the content on your site. A clear and organized site structure makes it easier for search engines to crawl and index your pages. This can improve your search engine rankings and make it easier for users to find your content.
2. It helps users navigate your site. A well-organized site structure makes it easier for users to find the content they want and can improve the overall user experience.
3. It can affect the loading speed of your site. A site with a large and complex structure may take longer to load, negatively impacting user experience.

Overall, a good site structure is essential for both search engines and users, as it helps to improve the accessibility and usability of your site.

With a good site structure, you will excellently plan the articles, and you can interlink the articles with one another to make your site easy for Google. This other way helps the reader to understand this better. Let's define this as a category, and we call it Face Makeup.

The ideal site structure:

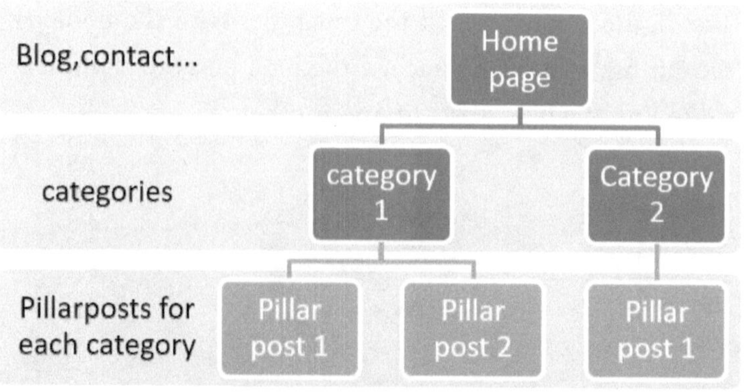

For creating your site structure, you have to define your categories. For example, let's consider our category as face Makeup.

I hope you got my drift.

One category must contain several linked blog posts.

These blog posts must be interlinked with one another. It will be easier for google to understand your site, and it will rank higher, and subsequently, you will get traffic.

In the first figure, I have linked the categories with the homepage, and in the second figure, I have attached the blog posts to the category and explained to link the blog posts to one another.

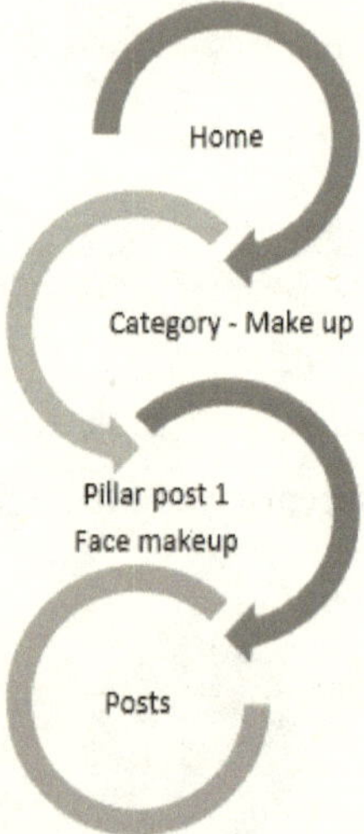

In a glimpse, merging both images,

I call this **Blogging flow!** The flow should keep running this way for the blog to stand out of the norm.

The final blog layout should be like this.

Whenever you schedule a post, you must prepare in this flow. You have to keep a content calendar and schedule the posts.

How to build a Content Inventory?

Determining your content containers may seem vague at this stage, but building your content inventory will set your boundaries to work. When you create your content inventory and target all of your content in clearly defined categories:

- You will be seen as an expert in a few topics rather than anything and everything.
- Your readers clearly understand what you are and what you write.
- You know what the next content you need to write is. Trust me; this is the best way to overcome writer's block.

I guarantee developing content inventory will take time to come. It takes time to find out what content resonates with your audience and also what your audience's interests are. These will shift over time, but it's good to have a rough sketch of your content boundary.

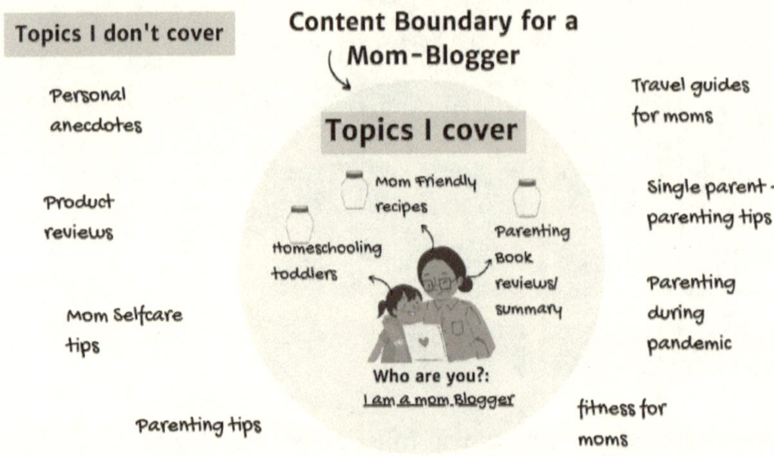

Consider Riya, a New Mom blogger; instead of overwhelming and asking everyone what to write, create a rough sketch of your content boundary like the one above, the topics you want to Cover and don't want to cover.

How to Capture Content Ideas?

It would help if you had a workspace like **Trello** or **Notion** to create a Content Inventory. Rather than going pen and paper, this enables you to view your progress. You can use my Free content calendar worksheet from the resources section to get started.

Method 1: Populate Ideas from your Niche:

You know about the Market ecosystem from chapter 2. If you have filled out the Niche Research workbook, you have noted a few of your competitors. Look at your competition. What worked well for them? Certain posts are evergreen. As you can see in the Blogging Niche, there will be a guide on "How to start a blog."

You can do this quickly and effectively with the help of SEO tools like Ubersuggest, Ahrefs and Semrush. But to get started initially, you can do it manually with search operators.

One search operator that can help you find popular posts within a particular niche is the "intitle" operator. This operator allows you to search for pages with a specific title word.

For example, if you wanted to find popular posts about parenting, you could use the following search query:

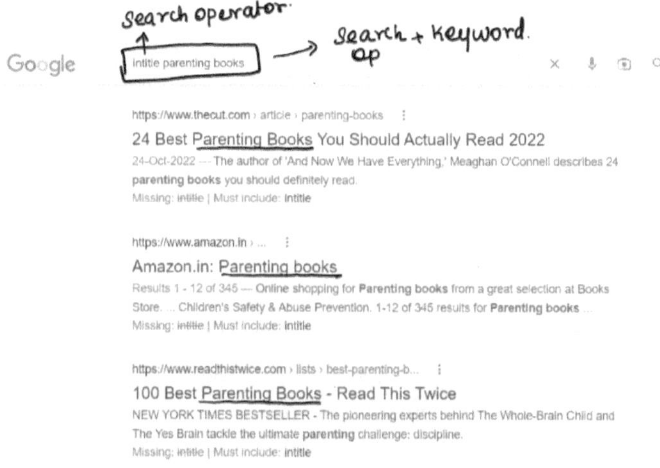

intitle: parenting

This would return a list of pages with the word "parenting" in the title. You can also use the "intitle" operator in combination with other search operators, such as "site", to narrow your results.

For example, if you only wanted to see results from a specific website, you could use the following search query:

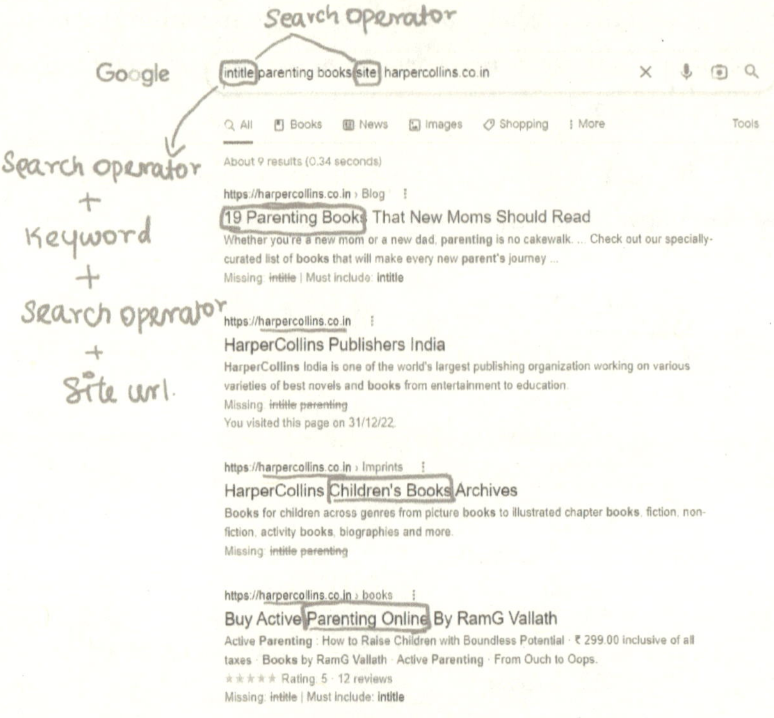

intitle: parenting site:www.example.com

This would return a list of pages with the words "parenting" in the title on the "**www.example.com**" website.

Here are some places where you can find content ideas:

- Pinterest
- Quora
- Reddit - Use the subreddit finder
- Facebook groups

You will get a bunch of content ideas to cover.

Method 2: Tools to create content calendar:

Apart from the paid SEO tools, You can use tools like

Answerthepublic and **Alsoasked** to generate content ideas. Hover over to the sites and enter your topic to get content ideas. Look at the image below from both sites.

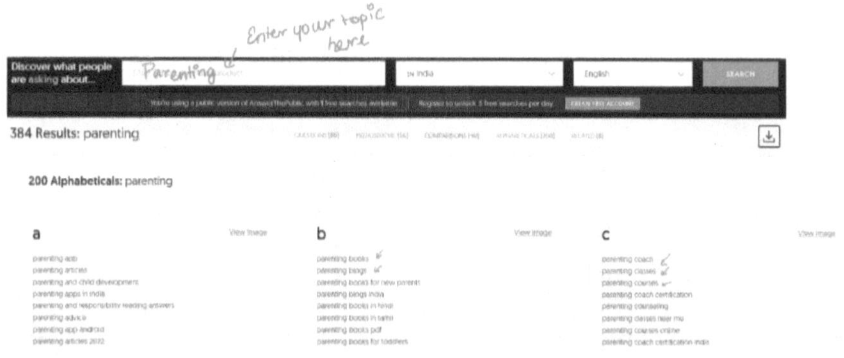

Alsoasked also show's different topics category wise

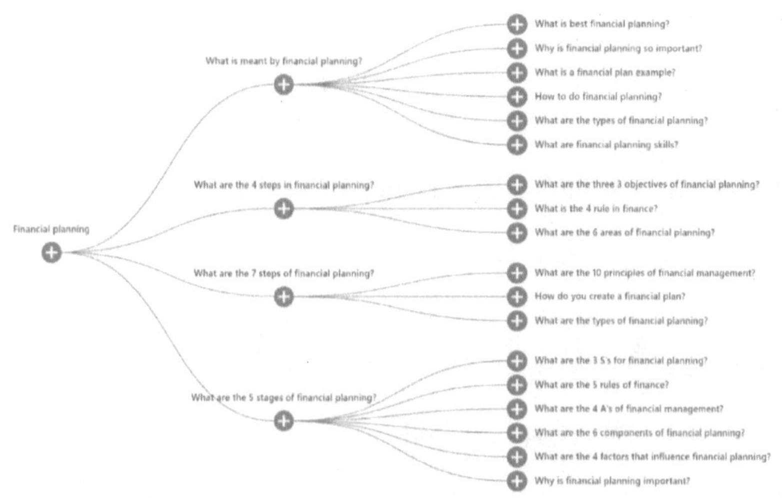

Method 3: Create content based on your reader's journey:

Talking about the reader's or customer's journey is an advanced topic. But I wanted to cover this one purposefully here. I teach about building blogging startups, which is why we think of blogs as problem solvers. Content marketers start with the customer journey, an important topic. Let's look at the customer's journey.

Everyone who reads your site is at a different awareness level. Some may be aware of the problem your product solves. Some may be actively searching for a solution. Others may not even know what's their problem.

Try getting an idea for the following questions.

- How does a customer buy a product?
- Can you sell so quickly?

Digital trends are updating.

Customers take time to buy things; they do a lot of research before getting things.

The best example:

What do you do before buying a mobile phone?

Do you go to Amazon, click on any mobile under 30K, add a cart, and order it?

Will you order the mobile in a fraction of a second?

Ultimately, the answer is **NO.**

Whoever may be reading this book may be a young college guy or a 40-year-old college lecturer.

The answer will be a desperate **NO.**

What do you do before buying a mobile?

Quickly think of the terms that come to your mind.

You will first **type in google.**

"best mobile under 30k"–You may check 2 to 3 mobiles

Now you have to choose which is best among them

You will now compare the models; for that, you will ask google

"OnePlus Nord 2T 5G Vs Google Pixel 6a, which is best?"

Now will be reading the lengthy technical terms provided by the experts.

Finally, you will decide to buy *the Google Pixel 6a.*

Then you will decide *where to buy this.* What are the offers provided by physical stores, and will you compare that with the online giant offers, amazon, etc.?

How long it will take to choose a product depends on the person deciding.

This is the **real scenery** behind every purchase, irrespective of the product.

That is why statistics say **44% of buyers** [28]say they typically consume three to five pieces of content before engaging with a vendor.

This digital media has created awareness among buyers. The bloggers who write content about the products spread their technical knowledge about the product.

Below is the typical buyer's journey.

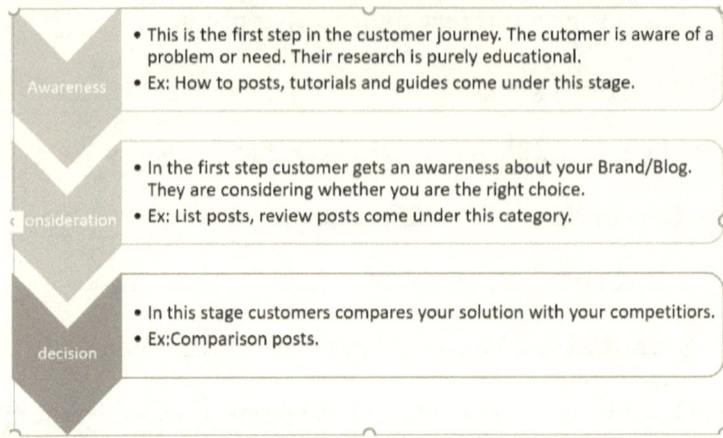

You may be thinking, why is this essential for me? I will write a blog post; why do I need to consider the customer journey?

The real reason behind mapping your content with the customer journey is to delight your readers and make them dwell in your blog.

Likewise to **start a review blog**, you have to plan your blog posts for every stage of your customer/reader.

Now you know what customers are doing before buying. Your goal is to construct a **conversion funnel that lines up with each step.**

Customers own the shopping experience; you are writing for their level.

How to map keywords with the customer journey?

Open the reader persona you created in the previous chapter.

Reader	Awareness	Consideration	Decision
Content types	Detailed explanation of the product	List of products matching their need	Comparison best products
Rita	How to apply a foundation cream?	List of foundation creams for dark skin	Loreal foundation vs lakme dark skin foundation cream
Ankur	How to earn money online?	30 sure fire ways to make money online	Create a blog or buy video lessons

It is now time to figure out what they want to see in each stage: awareness, consideration and decision.

Rita needs a foundation cream. After she had read the blog post on how to apply a foundation cream, she gained the confidence that everyone can apply foundation without patches. Then understood how to use a foundation flawlessly. Now she needs to buy a foundation to match her skin type, read a list of foundations, and finally purchase a product.

You have to understand and calculate what is in her mind and fulfil her needs to survive your business. This is what we call **a keyword funnel.** Likewise, Ankur wants to **earn money online** and wants to start a blog. He needs to gain technical skills. He knows blogging is a way to make money online. He is surfing the internet to understand how non-technical people are making. What would be his problems now? Think of his problems and write in a paper.

The problems may be,

- How to make money online?
- How to start a blog?
- What is WordPress? Why everyone recommends it?
- How to install WordPress plugins?

- Why should I use WordPress?
- How to write a blog post?
- What are the various methods of earning online?
- How to customize a WordPress theme?
- How to back up WordPress?
- How to automate email campaigns?
- How to add affiliate links to my posts?

Still, more questions will be there; now, let me show how to categorize the problems based on the user level and solve their issues.

Everything is based on the user persona. If you have not prepared one, kindly do it immediately. Only then will you understand the whole phenomenon.

Reader Stage	Problems	Solution	Blog post
Beginner	How to start a blog?	Step-by-step explanation to create a blog	How to start a blog in 2019
Beginner	How to install WordPress plugins	methods for installing a plugin	3 ways to install a plugin
Beginner	How to write a blog post	Blog post writing methodology	How to write a blog post in one hour
Intermediate	How to set up an email campaign	Use Mailchimp automation	An ultimate guide for using Mailchimp automation campaign
Advanced	How to outsource the blogging process	Places to find freelancers and methods of breaking the jobs into chunks	30 ways to batch your blogging process into manageable chunks

I have categorized the blog posts for each level in the above table. In the same way, you should cover each blog post. I have highlighted the keywords I used for each post.

This is how you can map the keywords for each blog post.

In quick steps:

Step 1: Define the content containers for your blog. You may have 3 to 5 content containers.

Step 2: Plan the pillar posts for each content container. You can plan any number of pillar posts for each content container.

Step 3: Brainstorm the posts for each pillar posts. Go to **Google Trends**, find what is trending now, and then plan for your posts. (optional)

Step 4: Create a content calendar for your blog and work based on that.

Step 5: Start writing the blog posts.

Step 6: Publish on time.

At the end of this chapter, you can find the workbook for Blogging flow. Download the workbook and fill it in before publishing your blog. This is the most crucial step in the overall blogging process.

How to fill the Blogging flow workbook:

Step 1: From the niche selection workbook you got in chapter 2, you have identified the competitor's in your niche.

Step 2: Scan at least 20 blogs in your niche and identify what they deal with.

Step 3: Try to find what is trending in their blog and check that with **Google trends**.

Step 4: Finalize your Categories and Pillar posts.

Step 5: Get an idea of five blog posts in at least one category.

Now that your content inventory is ready! Let's learn keyword research to rank your blog posts on Google.

Action Steps:

1. Download the content calendar template from the free resources.
2. Include every website/ competitor you found in the search.
3. Research the topics/ trending/seasonal topics in your niche
4. Create a content calendar based on your time availability.

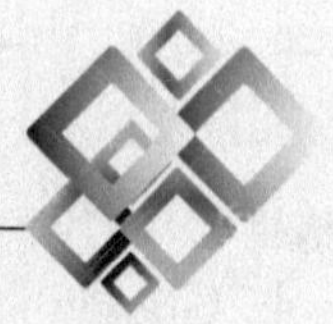

CHAPTER 6

THE KEYWORD MATRIX

Keywords everywhere!

Gone are those days when you could stuff keywords and rank your website.

Thanks to the intelligent search engine- Google!

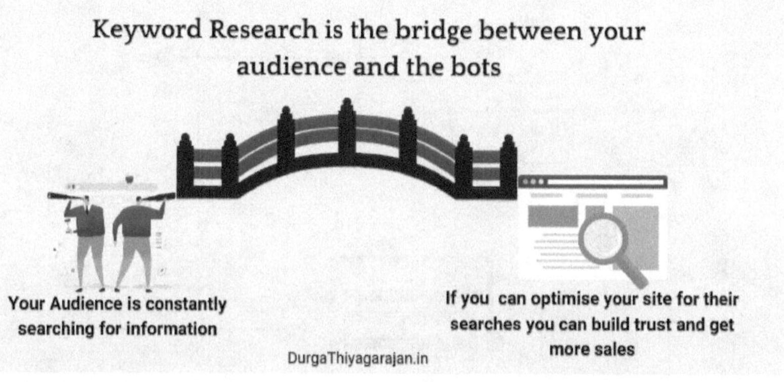

The unique smartness of google has brought quality articles worldwide. As a blogger, it is essential to write quality articles. At the same time, you need to understand your audience and try ranking for what they search.

"Keyword research helps you meet the two ends- writing for readers and optimizing for bots."

–Durga

How does google work?

One way to think about how Google works is to compare it to a library. Just like a library has a collection of books, Google has a collection of web pages. And just like a library uses a catalogue to help you find a specific book, Google uses an algorithm to help you find specific web pages.

When you go to a library and want to find a book, you might start by looking in the catalogue (which is essentially a list of all the books in the library, organized by subject). The catalogue tells you where to find the book on the shelves.

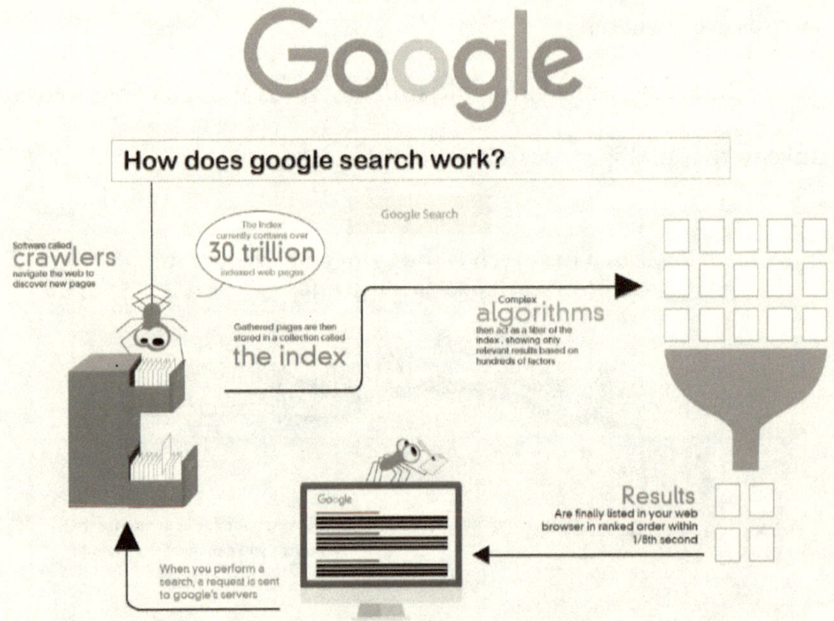

How google works Image[28]

Similarly, when you search for something on Google, you enter a keyword (e.g., "best coffee shops in New York"). Google's Algorithm looks through its index of web pages and returns a list of the pages that it thinks are the most relevant to your search query. The Algorithm determines a web page's relevance based on various factors, such as

- The page's content,
- The relevance of the page to the keyword,
- The quality of the website, and
- The overall authority and credibility of the website.

So, just like a library's catalogue helps you find a specific book, Google's Algorithm enables you to find specific web pages that are relevant to your search query.

The Algorithm is nothing but the bots programmed to do three essential functions crawling, Indexing and Ranking.

1. **Crawling:** Google uses automated software called "spiders" or "bots" to crawl and index the billions of web pages on the internet. These spiders follow links from page to page, reading and collecting information about each page they visit.
2. **Indexing:** As the spiders crawl and collect information about web pages, they add the information to Google's massive database of web pages, called the "index." The index is organized like a giant book, with each web page represented by a chapter.
3. **Ranking:** When a user searches, Google's Algorithm uses a number of factors to determine which web pages in the index are the most relevant and authoritative. The Algorithm then ranks the pages and displays the most relevant results first.
4. **Serving results:** When a user searches, Google's servers retrieve the most relevant web pages from the index and serve them to the user as a search engine results page (SERP). The SERP includes a list of web page titles, descriptions, and links to the pages.

This is a very simplified version of how Google works, and the actual Algorithm is much more complex and constantly evolving. However, this gives you a basic understanding of the process.

What is keyword research?

It is the process of finding the "phrases", "Terms", "and queries" that people are asking using a search engine.

We expect the search engine to give the results for our queries on the first page.

As a Blogger, you need to know what your readers are asking via search engines to optimize your blog pages and drive traffic to your blog.

Keyword research is finding valuable keywords that drive targeted traffic to the blog. You can identify readers' interest in a particular topic and find blogs like yours.

Benefits of Keyword research:

Google Search has become an integral part of our daily lives because it allows us to quickly and easily find the information we need. Whether we are looking for a specific piece of information, trying to find a local business, or just looking to kill time by browsing the web, Google Search is a go-to resource.

You are looking for an Answer to a problem. What will you do?

You **Google it.**

Right?

Most of us are always looking for a solution. Our queries maybe

1. To understand something
2. Find the solution to a problem
3. Find a store location
4. Buying a product
5. comparing two products

We expect Google to give us the solution on the first page of the search results. Most of us don't go beyond page 3 when looking for an answer.If you can reach the readers, you can grow your business.

How can you optimize your page for the query the reader is asking? The way of optimizing your content for the keywords is what we call **On-page SEO.**

Let's understand with an example,

You ask a query in google- What is Blogging?

While you are typing, you ask a query you want, or **google will help you ask the right questions by suggesting phrases related to what you are requesting.**

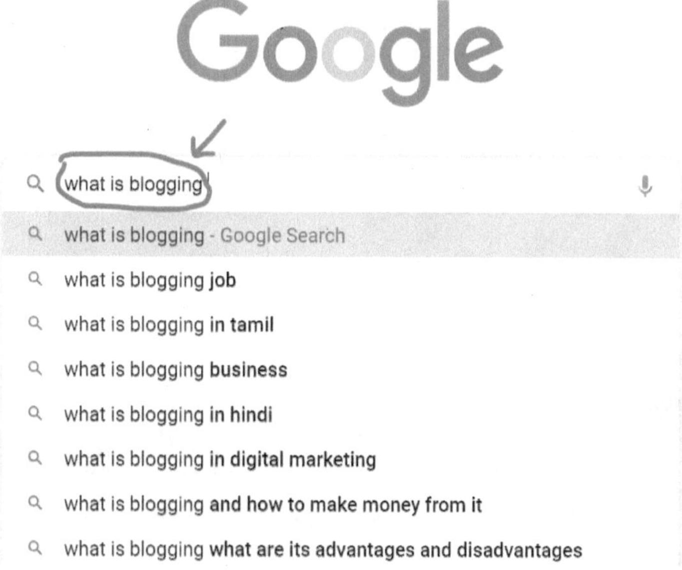

Look at the above image. You can find the autosuggestions by google for the question – What is Blogging?

Wondering, How are search engines suggesting?

Search engines like google will keep a log of users' queries worldwide. When you are typing a specific phrase, it will auto-suggest based on the previous searches by people worldwide. Trying to understand how google works will get you mad, so this guide is an actionable strategy to help you reach a targeted audience and rank your blog. The below image shows how to google autosuggestion works,

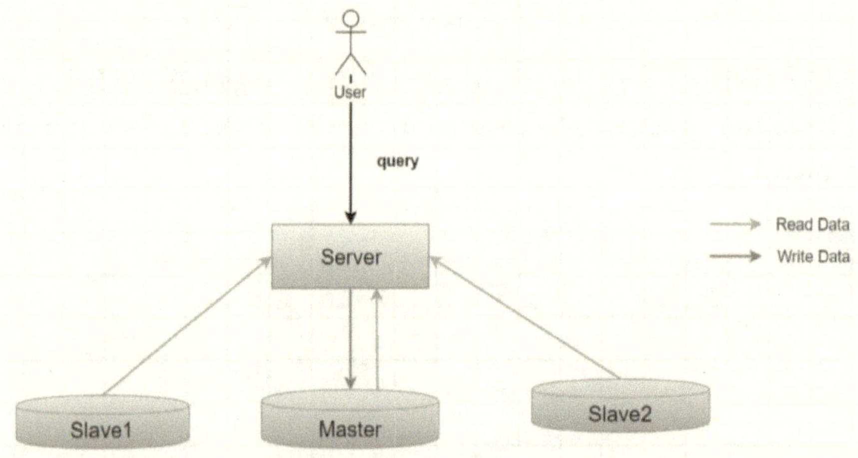

To simplify, let's continue.

The keyword research process will help you find the queries asked by users worldwide.

If you are building a blogging business or a content marketer, your primary role is to rank your page. In **that way, you can drive targeted traffic to your website.**

Now, let's find out how many people have asked this query: What is blogging?

The image below shows the search volume. I used google keyword planner for this.

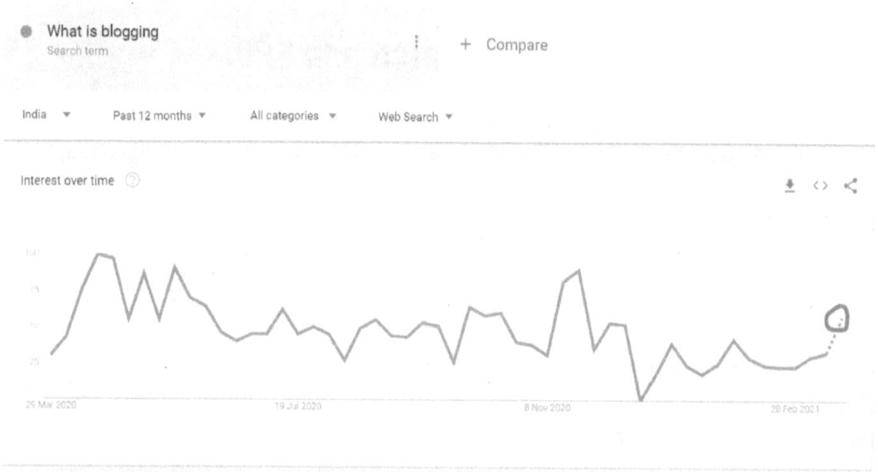

The above data says you can understand that *100k people are looking for a solution to this question.*

Let's dig more by finding how many Indians are asking this question on google. The image from Google Trends shows that around 58 people have asked this query while writing this book.

So, you have a handful of data now. I hope you learnt the importance of keyword research.

Let's summarise the benefits of keyword research.

1. **It helps you understand your audience:** Keyword research can give you insight into what people are looking for and how they are

searching for it. This can help you understand the needs and interests of your target audience and create content that resonates with them.

2. **It helps you optimize your website:** By using relevant keywords in your website's content, titles, and meta descriptions, you can make it more visible and appealing to search engines and users. This can help improve your search engine rankings and drive more traffic to your site.

3. **It helps you create content:** Keyword research can give you ideas for new content topics and help you create content that is more likely to rank well in search results.

Overall, keyword research is an important part of SEO because it helps you understand and connect with your audience, optimize your website, and create compelling content.

Keyword research and SEO:

Say you are a business blogger; you sell things online. It may be an Ebook or a course; if you know how to rank for a particular query, you can sell your products.

Keyword research helps in finding the targeted buyers for your product. This is what we call Inbound Marketing.

It means we are not searching for buyers. Instead, we are making ourselves stronger to let the buyers find us.

"Don't run behind the buyers; let them find you."

Types of keywords you need to know:

There are various types of keywords. Here I am not going to show the classes based on categories. Instead, I will share what a blogger needs to write better blog posts and drive traffic to a blog.

To build organic traffic to your blog, you need to know the core terms in your niche.

For example,

If you are into Fashion and Makeup, the **core terms** are like

- *Men's Fashion*
- *Women's Fashion*
- *Fashion designer*
- *Makeup artist*
- *Makeup products*

These are what we call **seed keywords**. These keywords are the baseline of your niche.

Seed Keywords:

Seed keywords are the most important word that represents your site. You want to rank for this keyword, but too many sites are already ranking. These are the high-search volume keywords. Most people are using and searching for this keyword.

They are also called **head keywords or short keywords, which** are very general and multi-purpose.

For Example:

You are in the Parenting niche,

Your core term or seed keyword is **"Parenting."**

You want to rank primarily for this primary term, but this, in general, is shared by most websites. The image below from ubersuggest shows this term's search volume and difficulty.

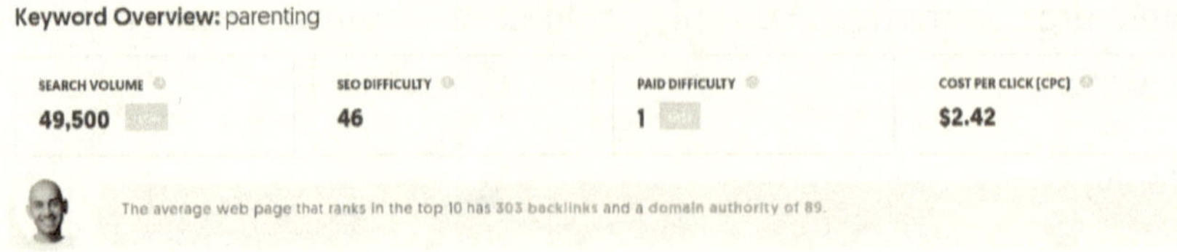

Why is it difficult to rank for seed keywords?

In simple words, seed keywords are single terms. Let's consider the keyword "Dog Food". The keyword "dog food" is shared by many websites that sell dog food, offer information about dog nutrition, or provide dog care tips. These websites include pet supply stores, pet food manufacturers, veterinary websites, and pet care blogs. Some examples of how the keyword "dog food" might be shared by these websites include:

- Pet supply stores might use the keyword "dog food" in their product titles and descriptions, as well as in their meta tags and alt text for images, such as "Organic Dog Food for Adult Dogs" or "Grain-Free Dog Food for Sensitive Stomachs."
- Pet food manufacturers might use the keyword "dog food" in the titles and bodies of their articles, such as "The Benefits of Feeding Your Dog a High-Quality Dog Food" or "How to Choose the Right Dog Food for Your Pet."
- Veterinary websites might use the keyword "dog food" in their articles, such as "The Importance of Proper Dog Nutrition" or "Common Mistakes to Avoid When Feeding Your Dog."
- Pet care blogs might use the keyword "dog food" in their posts, such as "The Best Homemade Dog Food Recipes" or "How to Read Dog Food Labels and Choose the Right Brand."

Using the keyword "dog food" in their content, these websites can attract visitors searching for information about dog food. However, because many websites use this keyword, it can be competitive, so it may be difficult for some websites to rank well for it in search engine results.

Look at the image below that compares the search volume of the three keywords - dog foods, dog foods for puppies and dog foods for puppy labradors.

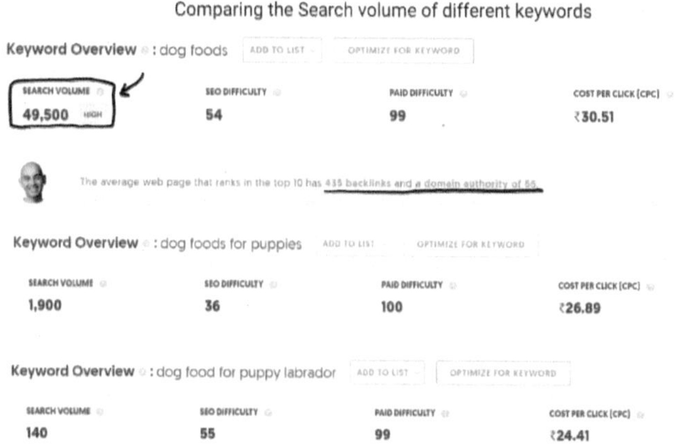

You can see the search volume is higher for the keyword dog food. It is because of two reasons,

1. Seed keywords are general, and they have a wide range of applications.
2. The competition is high because everyone wants to rank for this term.

The best thing you can do is derive the long tail keyword that caters for your business. You can do this by adding modifiers to the seed terms. Look at the image below; google auto-suggests the long tail versions.

Seed Keyword +Modifier = Business Keyword

It is your first-level niche keyword identification. Now let's compare the search volume of each keyword.

Seed Keyword	Modifier	Your First level Niche/Business
Parenting	Books	Parenting books
Parenting	Courses	Parenting courses
Parenting	tips	Parenting tips

Seed Keyword	Search volume	Modifier	First Level Niche keyword	Search Volume	Second level niche keyword	Search Volume
Parenting	60,500	Books	Parenting books	5,400	Parenting books for toddlers	1,900
Parenting	60,500	Courses	Parenting courses	590	Parenting courses online	320
Parenting	60,500	tips	parenting tips	1,900	Parenting tips for teenagers	190

As you see in the above table, the more modifiers I add, the search volume reduces, and the reach is unique to certain people.

Long-tail keywords:

If you dig deeper into this seed keyword, you will find that people who are interested in parenting are also interested in

- *styles of parenting*
- *parenting books*
- *parenting classes*
- and also questions like this,
- *Which parenting style is best?*
- *parenting with love and logic*
- *is parenting hard?*
- *Parenting with ADHD*

Long-tail keywords are **keywords that have three or more words**. They are usually more specific. They have a low search volume, and it targets the exact readers.

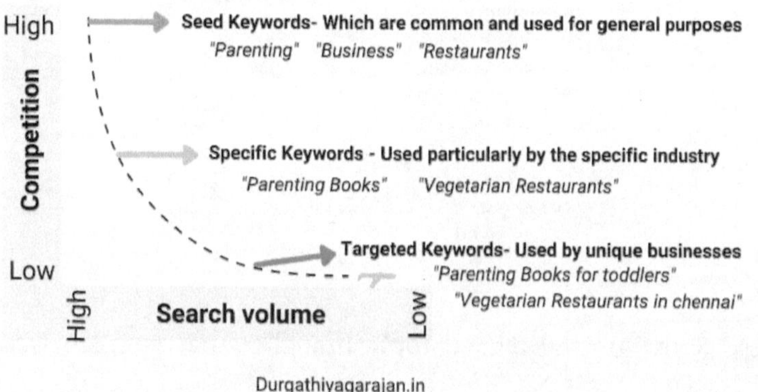

If you are someone selling parenting books, you need to target keywords like

- *Best parenting books for ADHD*
- *parenting books for toddlers*
- *Buy the whole brain child book online, etc*

The more specific you are, the higher your reach and the better your sales.

LSI keywords:

Latent semantic keywords are the thematic keywords related to your core term or the seed keyword.

If you are a food blogger and Baking is your niche,

then for the core term Baking,

The LSI terms are
- *cake*
- *bread*
- *bake a bread*

- *bake a cake*
- *cupcakes etc*

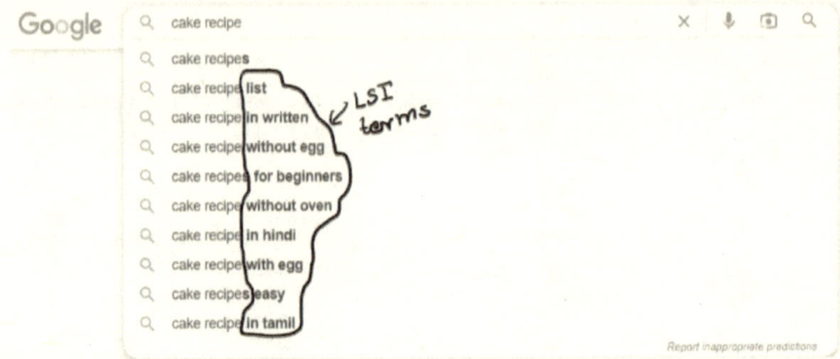

These terms are the related topic branches that you can write for. For example,

You can write

- *How to bake a cake*
- *How to make a bread*
- *Ten tips for making Christmas cupcakes etc.*

I hope you have an idea of the types of keywords. Now you need clarification about choosing a keyword for your blog post.

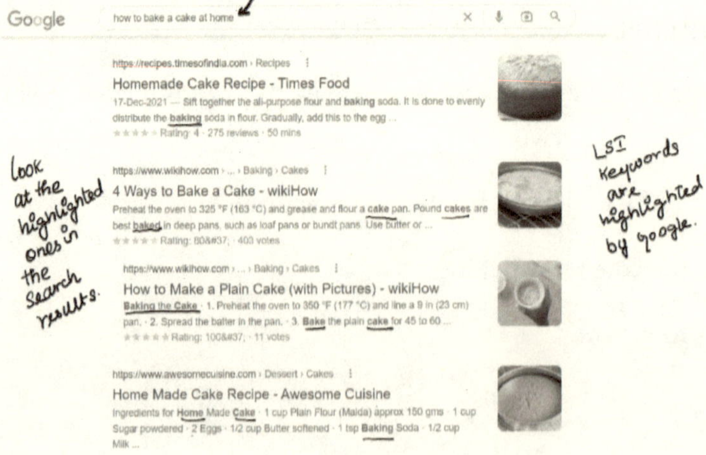

You can learn about LSI terms by entering your seed term in **Semantic-link.com**. Here is the search result for the term Baking.

Words semantically related to '**baking**' are:

breads	pastry	dough
bakers	oven	soda
baked	bake	cakes
roasting	bakeries	frying
ovens	pastries	cookies
bakery	bread	flour
bicarbonate	yeast	powder
pies	biscuits	cake
recipes	Loaf	Tartar
pans	powders	raisins

Stages of Keyword research

To write excellent blog posts, you need to know what people want. The first and the best advice is to know your reader. I mean your target audience. Your seed keyword is more generic and broad, as the name suggests. You are the only one who can tell the one term you want to rank.

If you are in the baking niche, baking is different from the primary term you want to rank. It would help if you niched down like,

- *Eggless Baking*
- *Baking bread*
- *Baking cakes*
- *Cake baking*
- *Cake baking recipe*
- *Cake baking tools*
- *Eggless cake baking*, etc.

This is what is the **keyword targeting structure**. This means adding the exact words to your core terms so that you represent yourself the best.

and still defining your content ideas like

- *How to bake a chocolate cake?*
- *How to bake a vanilla cake?*
- *How to bake a cupcake without eggs?*
- *10 things you need to bake a cake.*

As you see, the more and more questions I add, the more specific it is for the users.

Google is to find solutions to our queries. Your content strategy should cover the most questions in your niche and help people with various solutions. Long-tail keywords are the best way to find them. You can start evaluating the keywords if you have developed your content inventory with content containers.

3-Step Keyword Research Process:

Take some time to understand each stage. Make use of it.

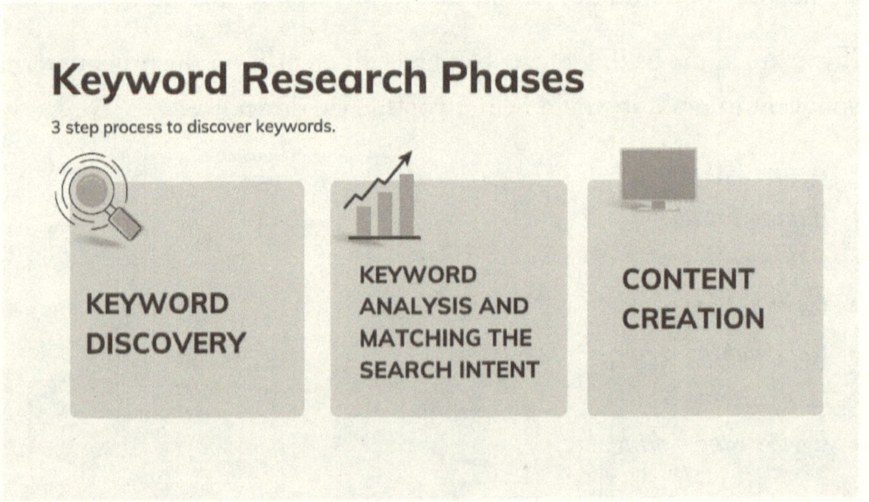

Stage 1: Finding the best keywords

To find keywords, you can use **google keyword planner** or any paid tools like **Uber suggest, ahrefs, semrush, keywordtool.io** etc.

The most important thing is to define your seed keywords.

Let's see how you can find your seed keywords.

I will explain this with various niches to get an overall idea about building a content strategy for your blog.

How to find the core terms/seed keywords?

You are best at defining that. You need to know.

- *What are you doing? – I am a digital marketing consultant*
- *What are the products you are selling?- I am selling digital marketing courses*
- *What words define your business?- Digital marketing expert, digital marketing consultant, and digital marketing coach. They are primarily teaching and consulting.*

The above ones are examples. You have to know who you are.

Another example in the Baking Niche,

- *Who are you? – I am a baking enthusiast. I like to teach Baking.*
- *What are you doing/ The products you are selling? – I sell cakes and bakery products online.*
- *What words define your business? Baking classes, Baking mentor, Buying cakes online etc.*

The rough estimate of keywords is ready.

Brainstorm the list of topics:

From the content containers you learnt in the previous chapter, brainstorm the topics you want to cover in your blog.

For a Baking Niche, the content containers may include

- Eggless Baking
- Pastry Recipes
- Cookies and Cupcakes
- Baking Tips

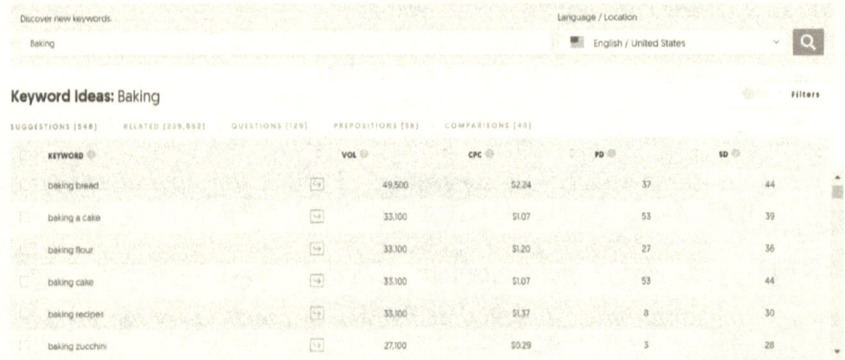

KEYWORD	VOL	CPC	PD	SD
baking bread	49,500	$2.24	37	44
baking a cake	33,100	$1.07	53	39
baking flour	33,100	$1.20	27	36
baking cake	33,100	$1.07	53	44
baking recipes	33,100	$1.37	8	30
baking zucchini	27,100	$0.29	3	28

And for a travel blog, look at the image below,

Ex: Travel Blogs

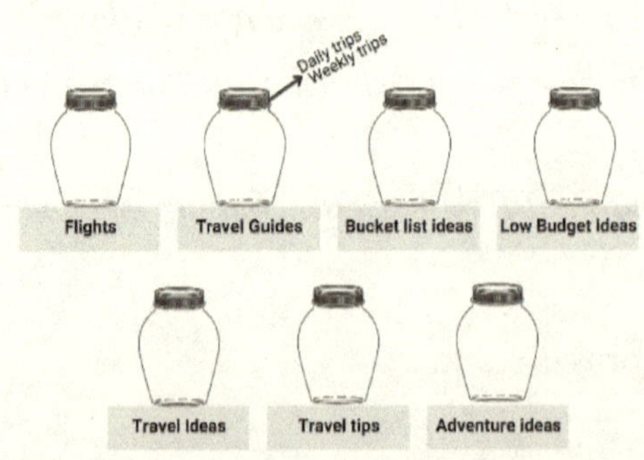

Related Searches:

When you type your seed query in google, you can find the related terms in the associated searches column.

For Baking, below are the related search results. I am assuming someone is interested in sharing baking recipes, so when you click on the baking recipes from related searches, you can find more long-tail versions.

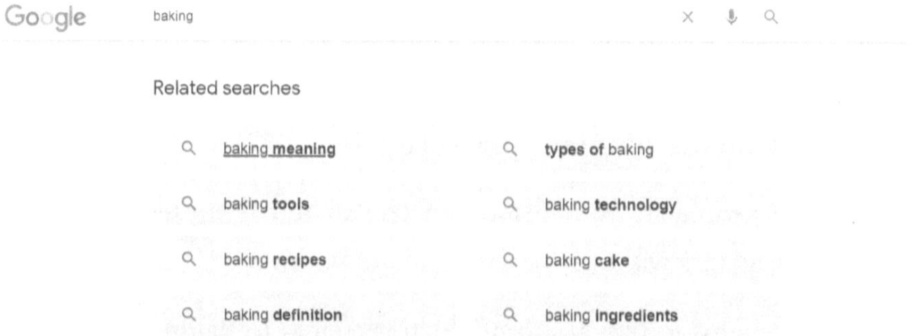

See the above image; you have a handful of topics. Choose them as you prefer and make a list.

Auto suggestions from Google, Pinterest, and Youtube:

Auto suggestions are the phrases that search engines automatically generate.

When I type Baking in google, I see the autosuggestions. These autosuggestions are based on the location.

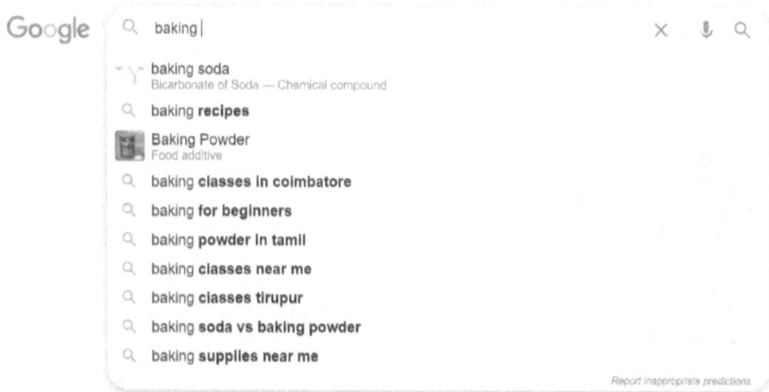

You can do the same with Pinterest and Youtube too. See, the auto suggestions are entirely different.

When you type in youtube, I use only the core term baking. If I use a specific word, baking cake, the search results are more detailed and accurate.

Let's find the long-tail keywords.

How to find the long tail keywords?

Seed keywords have a high search volume. This means there are a lot of people who are searching for a particular term.

Only some people are your readers. If you share baking recipes, people looking for recipes will only be interested in your blog.

If someone wants to buy an oven(which is related to Baking), they don't consider your blog. This way, long-tail keywords help to filter your readers.

Let's see how you can find the long tail versions for your seed keyword.

Think of long-tail versions as the query they type in google. If you know the fundamental questions in your niche, then that is the long tail keyword.

From the above method of autosuggestions from Google, Pinterest and Youtube, if I use a specific keyword, "baking cake", you can find the below result.

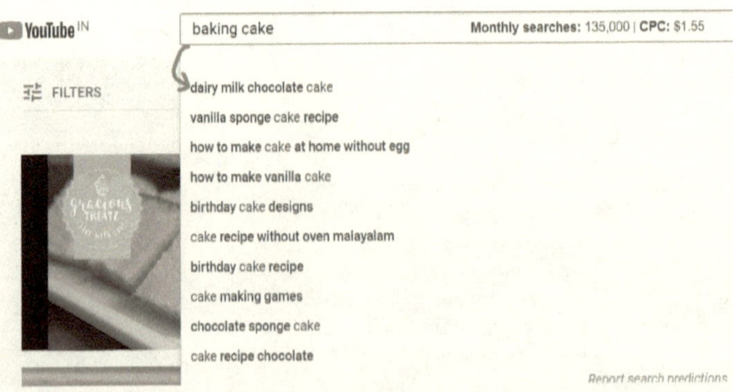

Even this keyword has a high search volume of 135,000 per month.

Let's cook for the search volume of

- *vanilla sponge cake*
- *how to make vanilla cake*
- *birthday cake designs etc*

Let's say I want to make a vanilla cake, the autosuggestions from youtube,

YouTube IN

how to make vanilla cake

FILTERS

UPLOAD DATE   TYP

Last hour   Vid

Today   Cha

This week   Pla

This month   Filn

This year   Pro

how to make vanilla cake **at home**

how to make vanilla cake **without egg**

how to make vanilla cake **in microwave**

how to make vanilla cake **without oven**

how to make vanilla cake **in malayalam**

how to make vanilla cake **at home without oven**

how to make vanilla cake **in tamil**

how to make vanilla cake **eggless**

how to make vanilla cake **in oven**

how to make vanilla cake **with egg**

how to make vanilla cake **at home without egg**

how to make vanilla cake **without vanilla essence**

how to make vanilla cake **in cooker**

how to make vanilla cake **at home in tamil**

See the autosuggestions from youtube; if you can relate to the previous auto suggestions, this one seems much better and valuable. You can figure out the exact keyword you want.

Note: You can try doing the same autosuggestions test in Google, Pinterest and Bing and make a list of useful long-tail keywords to write a blog post.

In the next stage, I will show you how you can validate the long tail versions and find the untapped keywords where you can rank for.

Using Answer the Public tool:

Another interesting tool is the **Answer the public**. It takes time if you are looking for autosuggestions from search engines. This tool summarises the queries and consolidates them into an extensive, helpful list.

Look at the below image; These are the queries people actively seek answers to. Answer the public is free for three searches and has a paid version.

This way, you can find a list of topics to write content on. You can fill your content calendar with these questions and start writing content.

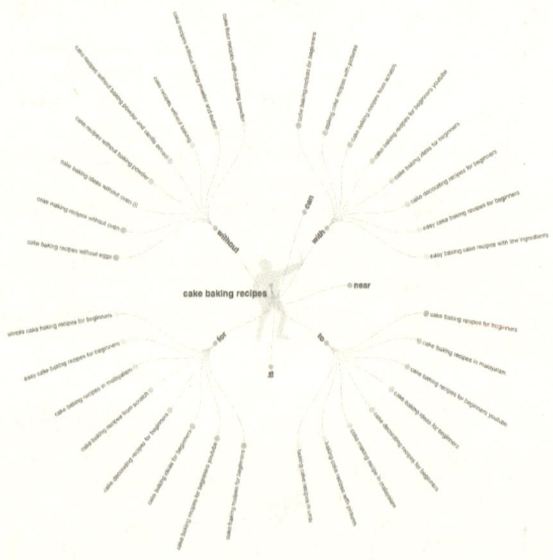

Also asked Questions from Google:

Another way to find the long-tail keywords are from the also-asked section of google. This gives you data on what people are looking for while searching for a query.

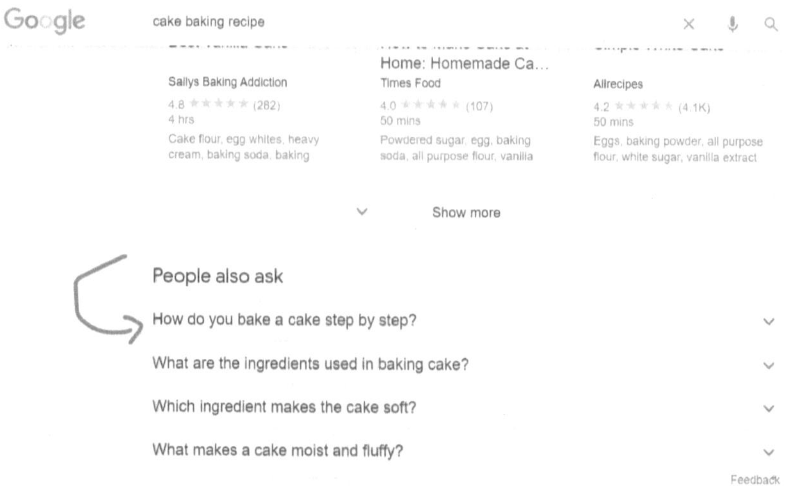

You can either write a new post on each. Or you can write answers to these questions in a blog post.

Google says that people looking for cake recipes want answers to the following questions.

- *How do you bake a cake step by step?*
- *What are the ingredients used in baking a cake?*
- *Which ingredient makes the cake soft?*
- *What makes a cake moist and fluffy?*

When you are writing a blog post on a specific cake, say, for example, vanilla cake. You can include all the questions in your blog post.

Questions from Quora, Reddit, and Forums:

Quora is a gold mine for bloggers and content marketers. You can find out what your readers are asking and the answers they are getting.

Check the below image,

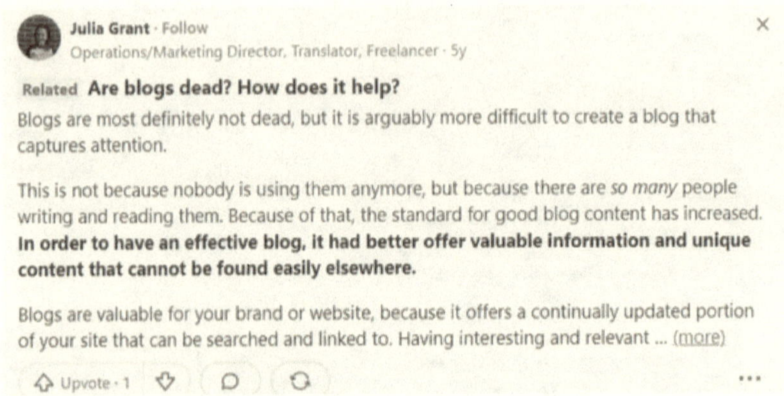

I hope you got a lot of ideas for your content. Make a list of topics found from the above methods. We will be evaluating the keywords in the second stage of keyword research.

> **Note:** Choose as many keywords as you want. You can use the long-tail keywords as the secondary keywords for your blog posts.

How to find LSI keywords?

When writing a blog post, you will already be using LSI keywords. To avoid keyword stuffing, Google introduced LSI keywords as a ranking strategy. Until and unless you don't stuff keywords, you need not worry about the LSI keywords.

For example,

Imagine you type a specific query- How to decorate a cake

You open a blog post on the first page, with only pictures with keywords stuffed.

Will you be happy?

NO!

That's why LSI keywords are there. Let's find it with a tool.

Using Twin word LSI finder:

Go to **Twinword LSI finder** and enter the seed keyword, and you will get the words you need to use in your blog post.

Like the below image,

Popular Topics	Keyword	AVG. Monthly Searches	SEO Competition	Paid Competition	Keyword Score	Title Score	Relevance
mary berry (20)							
chocolate cake (18)	decorated cake	49,500	15	100	★★		
cake decorating (14)	cake baking	33,100	16	54	★★		
sallys baking addiction (13)	cake making	33,100	16	17	★★★★	★★★	
carrot cake (12)	tube pans	9,900	16	100	★		
banana cake (11)	cooling cake	8,100	16	91	★		
$ Affiliate program	oreo cheesecake no bake	8,100	11	9	★★	★★★	
Have feedback?	wilton cake pans	8,100	13	100	★		

You reached the end of stage 1 of finding the keywords for your blog post.

If you have followed me step by step, you might have a list of keywords in your hand. Let's evaluate each keyword and find a keyword to write a blog post.

Stage 2: Evaluating the keywords:

There are several factors to consider when evaluating a keyword:

1. **Relevance:** Is the keyword relevant to the content on your website? If not, it might not be a good keyword to target.

2. **Search volume:** How many people are searching for the keyword? If the search volume is low, it might not be worth targeting the keyword, as it might not bring much traffic to your website.

3. **Competition:** How many other websites are using the keyword? If the competition is high, it might be difficult for your website to rank well for the keyword.

4. **Target audience:** Is the keyword being used by your target audience? If not, it might not be a good keyword to target.

So we are going to analyze our content calendar.

Before that, you need to know the basic keyword metrics.

Basic Keyword Metrics you need to know:

1. **Keyword search volume:** The number of people searching for a particular keyword in a month. Keywords with high search volume mean a lot of demand, which makes it challenging to rank for. Keywords with a low search volume of <50 are like wasting time. They might gain popularity over some time.

2. **Keyword difficulty:** The score ranges from 0-100 for how difficult it is to rank a keyword. You have to aim for low-difficulty keywords. If the keyword difficulty is above 50, most brands are objective for that particular keyword. If you are a beginner, start with something other than big brands. Try ranking for low-difficulty keywords, and you can target difficult keywords at a later stage.

3. **Competition:** It is similar to keyword difficulty. It is used in the google keyword planner. Most paid tools use the term keyword difficulty, while keyword planner uses the word competition.

4. **Ad impression share:** This is for AD experts.

With the metrics known, do you know why 135,000 people are searching for a particular term? What is the intention behind their search?

Let's see that so that we can write better blog posts.

Learn to match your keyword with the search intent:

What is search intent?

If you are probably confused with this new term, then here is an example for you,

If you want to buy an oven, what will you type in Google?

It's likely to enter these keywords:

- *Best oven*
- *Best oven for Baking*
- *Ovens for baking 2020*
- *Best Microwave ovens under 20000*
- *Bosch oven*
- *IFB oven*

Now ask yourself, Why did you enter these keywords? With a motive to buy or find information regarding a particular product?

This is what we call search intent.

Search intent refers to the purpose behind a search query. When someone types a question or phrase into a search engine like Google, they are looking for something specific - an answer, a solution, information, etc. The search engine's job is to understand the intent behind the search and return the most relevant results.

For example, if someone searches for "best restaurants in New Delhi," their intent is likely to find a list of recommended restaurants to try in New Delhi.

On the other hand, if someone searches for "how to make a Vegetable salad," their intent is probably to find a recipe or tutorial for making a Vegetable salad.

In keyword research, it's important to understand search intent because it helps you create content that will actually be useful and relevant to the people searching for specific keywords. If you create content that aligns differently from the search intent of the keywords you're targeting, it's likely to rank well in the search results and may not be helpful to the people who find it.

For example, if you're trying to rank for the keyword "best restaurants in New Delhi" but your content is about the list of restaurants in New Delhi, it's unlikely to be what the searcher is looking for, and they are likely to leave your site quickly.

On the other hand, if your content is a curated list of the best restaurants in New Delhi, it's more likely to satisfy the searcher's intent and keep them on your site longer.

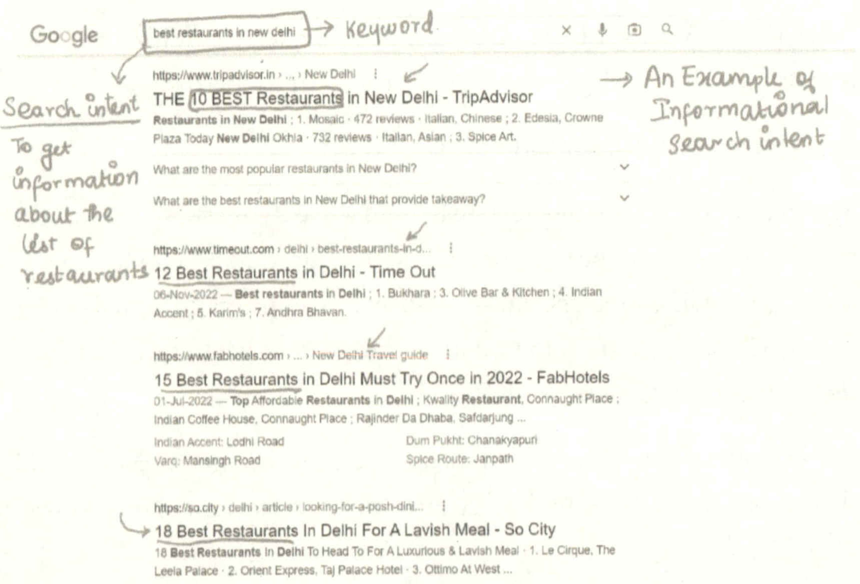

This is how Google displays the results for a specific keyword. Every search result page matches the search intent of the keyword.

Types of search intent and matching keywords with them:

There are generally four types of search intent:

1. **Informational:** When someone seeks information or knowledge on a specific topic. Examples of informational searches include "What is the capital of France?" or "How does a car engine work?"

2. **Navigational:** When someone is looking for a specific website or webpage. Examples of navigational searches include "Facebook login" or "Amazon homepage."

3. **Transactional:** When someone is looking to purchase or take another specific action. Examples of transactional searches include "Buy Nike shoes online" or "Renew driver's license."

4. **Commercial investigation:** When someone is considering purchasing but still gathering information and comparing options. Examples of commercial investigation searches include "Best laptop for college students" or "Electric toothbrush reviews."

Understanding the different types of search intent can help you create more relevant and valuable content for those searching for specific keywords. For example, you create an informational article about the history of chocolate. In that case, it's more useful to someone searching for information on the topic rather than someone looking to buy chocolate. Few more examples for the search intent types,

Informational – A person is looking for information or knowledge upgrade. Which means they want an immediate answer or a solution to their problem.

Example:

- *What is a blog post?*
- *How to write an article?*
- *Indian president name*

- CSK vs SRH (Every Indian knows this abbreviation! and we use this a lot, many times)

The above keywords have a purity of knowing something. This is called informational search intent. You can check the results for these keywords will be article pages. Sometimes, google displays the Answer on the search results page itself.

Navigational – A person is trying to reach a site. They know what they want instead of copying paste the complete site address. They are trying to enter the site name.

Example:

- *Facebook*
- *Youtube login*
- *Apple store*
- *iPhone 12 purple Flipkart*

The above keywords have a search intent of going to a known destination. The results will be the product pages.

Look at the microwave example I have shown.

Transactional and Commercial- When someone is trying to buy something, they research by comparing products. These searches are purely transactional.

For example:

- buy iPhone 12 purple online
- buy microwave oven
- Ubersuggest demo

These keywords are to buy something, and Google will display only the product pages.

Now let's match the keywords with the search intent:

As a blogger, you must reach your content for most informational searches. If you are selling some digital products or courses, you need to rank for navigational and transactional keywords.

You have a good idea of matching the keywords with the search intent. When writing content, compare it with the user's search intent.

S.No/Keyword intent	Informational	Transactional	Navigational
1	What is On page SEO	Best On-page SEO course	SEO course by XXXX
2	How to find a headline score?	headline studio demo	headline studio by coschedule
3	How to make a vanilla cake	Buy birthday cake online	vanilla cake by xxxxx

Another best example is the keyword - "How to lose weight". The search intent of the keyword "how to lose weight" is informational. Someone searching for this keyword is probably looking for information on how to lose weight, such as tips, techniques, or advice on achieving their weight loss goals. They might be interested in learning about different weight loss methods or seeking guidance on creating a healthy and sustainable weight loss plan.

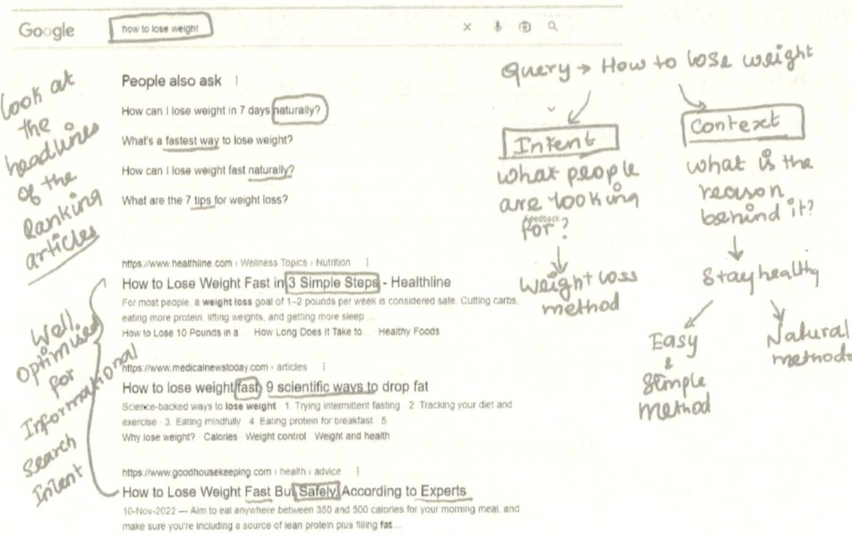

Once you understand your readers, as discussed in the previous chapter. You can write well-optimized articles just like the above ones. To decode this one much better, most people looking for weight loss methods want safer, natural and easy ways, which is why these trigger words are found in the headlines of the articles.

Use Google keyword planner to evaluate the keywords:

You might have a list of keywords to write. Let's evaluate the keywords and find the best keyword to rank.

You will evaluate the keyword based on the following metrics.

What is the estimated traffic?
- *How tough is it to rank for the keyword?*
- *How many people have searched for the keyword?*
- *How well can you compete with the ranking sites?*

Let's do that with Google Keyword Planner. You can use tools like Ahrefs, Semrush and Ubersuggest to get more accurate and well defined metrics.

Step 1: Go to **google keyword planner**

Step 2: Enter the keywords list you have prepared in the first step.

Step 3: Refine your search and download the keyword ideas.

I am going to use the one I prepared for a financial blog in the previous chapter.

Once you obtain the results like the above, you can download the csv and analyse that manually on MS-Excel or Google Sheets.

Here's a screenshot of the ubersuggest output

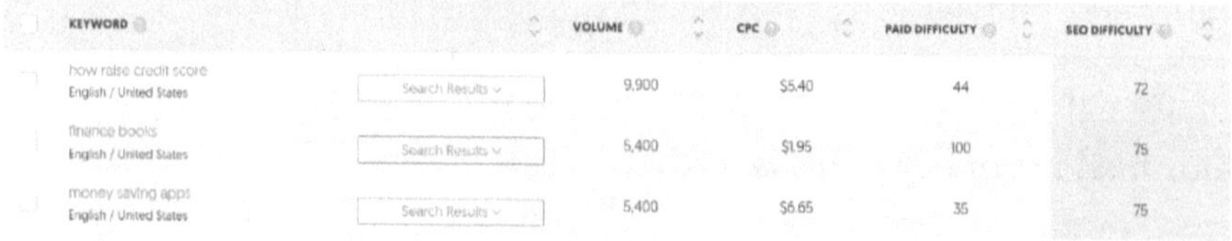

The paid tools give you everything like what's ranking and the content ideas for a keyword.

So entering only the informational keywords from the above list. Look at the image below. What is our overall goal of keyword research now?

Your goals can be

- Building your brand awareness
- Educate your audience

- Showcase your product
- Get leads for your service.

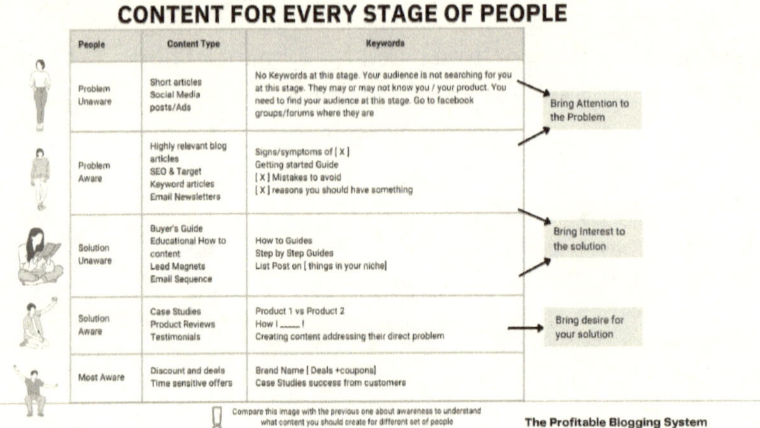

The best keywords for small sites or beginner sites –

Go for high search volume and low competition keywords. You need to rank for the standard competition keywords when you are just starting. Later, you can shift your focus to medium and high-competition keywords. I highlighted the keywords with low competition and high search volume in the above image.

Figure out the primary and secondary keywords for your blog post. Now your final list of keywords is ready!

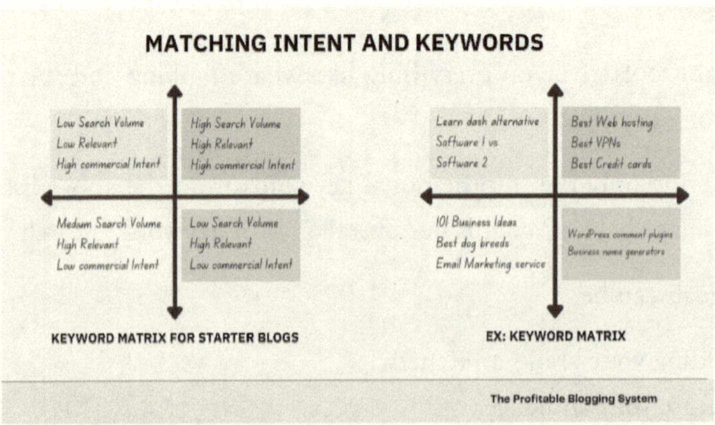

Let's see how you can use them in blog posts.

Stage 3: Using Keywords in a blog post:

Most people want to know the on-page optimization. But the real effort of on-page SEO comes with efficient keyword research. When you choose the right keywords, you can use them in your blog posts effectively.

Primary keyword optimization:

Now the primary keyword is your target keyword.

The primary keyword must be used in

The title of the page – H1 tag

In the URL of the page

In the first paragraph of the content

In one of your subheadings – the H2 tag

In the alt tag of an image

In the meta description

You can easily do this with your SEO plugin. Let me show you an example.

How to optimize the URL and title of the blog post with the primary keyword?

Step 1: Install the rank math plugin.

Step 2: After writing an article in the rank math settings, click on the edit snippet.

Step 3: Write the title you want to appear on the search result page. Your display title can be different from the one you want to appear in the search results.

Rewrite the blog post URL with the primary keyword and include a primary keyword in the meta description.

This is how you can optimize your content with the primary keyword.

Secondary keywords in the content:

Secondary keywords play a role in ranking the various keyword. A single blog post can rank for multiple keywords. Consider using your secondary keyword throughout your blog post and in sub headings (h1 & h3). This way, you can rank for as many keywords as possible.

> ## Action Steps:
>
> 1. Download the Keyword research workbook from the Free resources.
> 2. Refine the keywords you found for each topic.
> 3. In the content calendar you prepared in the last chapter, fill in the keywords you use for each topic. Write the primary and secondary keywords you want to target for the article.

CHAPTER 7

THE CONTENT CREATION

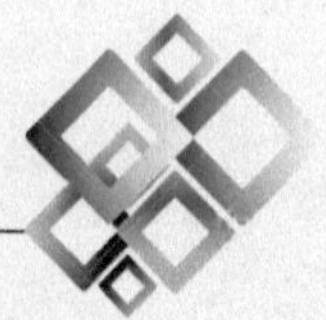

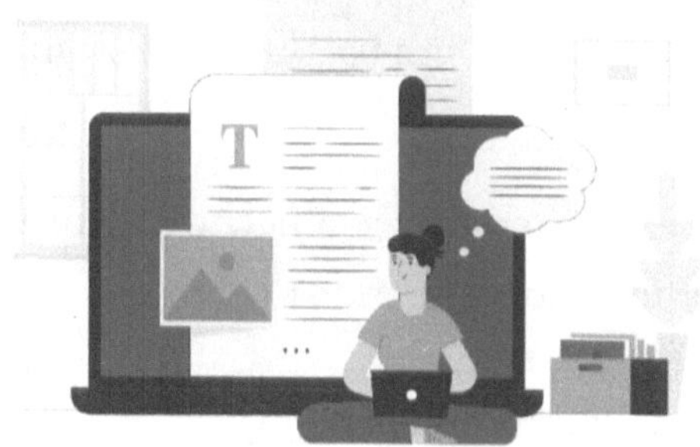

*W*hat are the elements of a perfect blog post? Whether it's 2022 or 2023, writing stays the same over the years. If you ever wonder how top-performing bloggers publish unique content, this chapter on writing a blog post is for you.

If you are someone Who sits to write with a blank screen open, With multiple tabs opened to find words to start, Then you need to know that, Talented writers have a process for writing a blog post. It is the secret behind their work efficiency and their content production.

For most writers, writing without a precise workflow wastes time and takes all your energy.

To produce quality content in a long row, you need a blog writing process to create more content in a brief span.

Whether you are a blogger who wants to build a blogging business or a content writer in a marketing team, this method can get you results with little planning. This process is simple and easy to follow, Here's how to write blog posts that stand out and drive audience attention.

Elements of a perfect blog post

Over the last five years of blogging, I have read blogs of eminent bloggers and realized something important for every blogger. They all have a structure for writing a blog. While the blog post structure may vary from one person to another, I am confident that they follow a pattern in writing the blog posts. They all follow a blog writing process that helps them to stand out from the crowd. Grab the reader's attention and resonate with them. Writing a good blog post is understanding the various elements of a blog post. Once you know, you can reproduce them with your unique style.

Every writer, maybe a new writer or you are writing for years, to tackle writer's block, here are the few essential things that I want to share:

Plan your time to:

- Discover the ideas
- Sketch them into a structure
- Write a draft that lets the readers travel in a flow.

These tips ensure that you are writing for the readers. I use this process to write every blog post.

Here are the nine elements of a blog post:

- The Content calendar preparation
- Keyword Research and matching with the search intent
- Preparing an outline for your blog post
- Writing headlines that grab the attention of the readers
- Introduction that hooks the readers

- A captivating story that energies readers to read
- A crafty closure
- Adding images that convey the essence of the blog
- Editing and proofreading like a pro.

Out of the nine elements, you should have created your content calendar in the last chapter. Once you clearly know what you will write, you can avoid writer's block. With that in mind, I include the blog post template here. As the image shows, a blog post needs all these elements to stand out online.

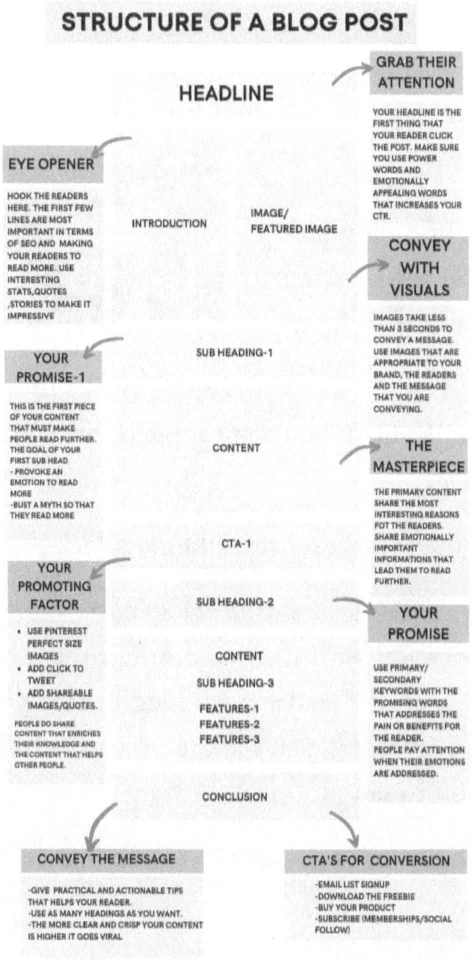

Before writing a blog post, the first and foremost thing is to know your audience.

Get to know your audience

"Write to please just one person"- Kurt Vonnegut.

Of course, every blogger wants thousands of readers for their blog posts. I may limit to thousands; you can imagine a million readers for your blog.

Okay, does every reader feel you have written a blog for them? That never happens,

The real essence of a blog post is to enchant the reader. Your target audience wants to know that,

You empathize with them; you want to help them Make them feel that you write for them.

You understand their fears, dreams, and roadblocks.

Visualizing one reader makes your blog posts more vivid and more personal. This connects with them and brings them back to your blog. It's a mission wherein the reader must long to read your blog posts. To deliver value to your readers, you want to provide what they want to hear, not what you want to say.

Do you know what your target audience is curious to know?

No?

Then it's time to stop here and find out what your target audience wants.

Anyone can do keyword research, find trending content online, and write. But not everyone can tap and connect with the readers. So if your journey is like a marathon to influence your readers, you must understand them.

Here is the list of questions to brainstorm what your ideal readers are looking for:

- *What is the most critical roadblock preventing my readers from achieving what they want to achieve?*
- *What are the long pressing questions that run through their mind?*
- *What goals do they have?*
- *What are they focusing on right now?*
- *What satisfies them more?*
- *When opening this blog post, what will they look for?*

Below is the template I personally use to note down my audience. I use a three-step method.

Ask yourself these seven questions and take time to figure out your sketching plan for your blog post.

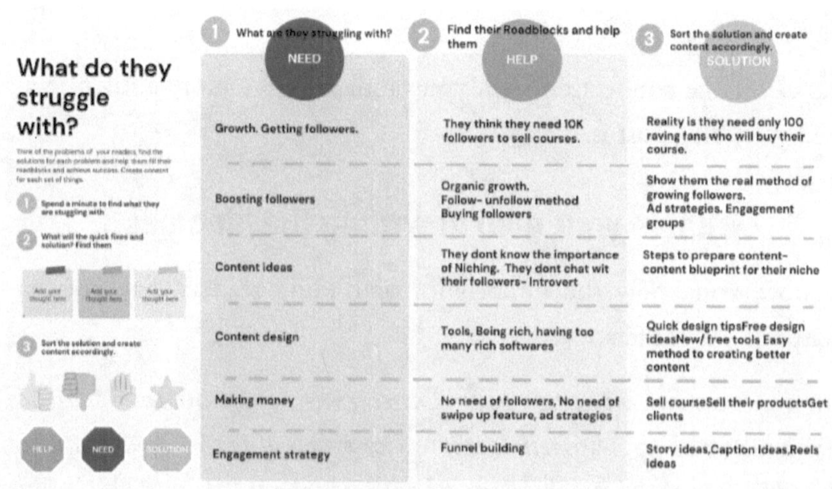

You can download the expanded and clear version of the copy from the bonus page.

Let's deepen finding your target audience with the following techniques:

Survey your readers: Every blogger uses social media to build their influence. You can ask your followers direct questions on social media. If you have a separate FB group, you can start polls, ask questions, etc. On Instagram, you can use stories to ask what your readers want from you. I connect with my readers on Instagram and find the topics for my next blog post.

Find from Google Auto suggestions: It is the best way to identify the readers' needs. When you type your query on Google, it suggests what people are searching for.

Find from FB groups: Find the top groups in your niche. Deep dive into the insights and discover what your readers are most likely looking for. Take a list of things you need to cover in the article and finally use them in your content.

Explore Quora and Reddit for the trending questions: You can find many questions in different formats here. Before writing every article, look at Quora for additional queries and top-rated answers to dig into the reader's mind. Same, you can use it for Reddit.

The closer the connection with your audience, the more authentic and vivid your blog post is.

What is your goal in writing the blog post:

By now, you know the importance of finding readers. Say you have identified the readers,

You want to share *investing tips for Entrepreneurs of age 30(Your audience)*, or you may wish to share *retirement tips for people of age 50(Your Audience)*. You can't match the expectations of both people on the same blog. Even though there is an interconnection between the investment at the age of 30 and the retirement at 50, the expectations don't meet the end.

Now it's time to figure out the *purpose of your blog.*

Your objective of blogging is to get more sales for your products.

Get website traffic, and increase brand awareness. Or to showcase yourself as an authority in your niche.

What is the goal of your Blog post?

Substantial Goal

- Promote your email list.
- Lead them to buy your product or service.
- Make an affiliate commission.
- Pitch a sponsored post.
- Educate your reader (how-tos).

You can analyse the success rate of these goals.

Insubstantial goal

- To position yourself an authority in your niche
- Network with influencers (through a roundup post).
- Entertain with personal stories.

You can't predict the success rate of these goals.

Durgathiyagarajan.in

If your blog is just a sales pitch, it will be hard to reach your audience, and your blog may remain a lonely voice while no one pays attention to it.

Most people aren't interested in your sales messages. They don't even want to know what business you are doing. They are interested in what is there for them.

"To build a business with your blog, stop thinking like a salesperson using a witty sales technique and start helping your readers and becoming their mental mentor."

–Durga

In promoting your business essentials, such as growing your email list or promoting your products or service, *you need to make sure you are educating/helping your readers.*

How to define the purpose of the blog post?

To clearly define the purpose of the blog post, ask yourself these questions.

Why am I writing this blog post? When defining your why, the answer must come from your heart. Clearly, from the perspective of a mentor or an inspirer. Your why statements can be like this –

I want my readers to understand the email marketing basics so that it helps them to choose a better email service provider.

I want my readers to realize the importance of keyword research to amplify their SEO efforts.

What do I want my readers to do after reading the blog post? So you have written a lengthy blog post of 2000 words or more. Do you want your readers to exit the blog? You might have spent 5 hours writing; what is your desired ROI? Your what statements are like

I want my readers to sign up for my email list to get my Free email marketing checklist and increase my subscribers.

I want to make my readers buy my affiliate product-xxxx

How do I want my readers to feel after reading the blog post? Ultimately, your readers should have a specific feeling that makes them want to return for more. So how do you want your readers to feel at the end of the blog post? Your How statement can be like this.

I want my readers to feel they have upgraded their knowledge of email marketing.

I want my readers to learn about various products.

9 Step process for writing a blog post

With the knowledge of understanding the target audience and matching it with the business goals, we will see the actual process of writing a blog post. Understanding only the blog post structure can't help you create more authentic content in the long term. You will learn how to write a blog post from the very basic brainstorming and research process.

Let's begin,

Step 1: Create your content calendar:

You may have a bucket list of blog post ideas. If you are someone new and need to learn about creating a content calendar, this is the first thing you should do.

For example,

You are writing eight different articles on Foundation creams. If your keyword is Foundation Cream and your blog posts are

1. Best *Foundation cream* for dark skin.
2. How to apply a *foundation cream.*
3. Top-quality *foundation creams* within 1K.
4. Best-ever deals for *foundation creams* in Amazon 2019.
5. Is cream *foundation* better than liquid?
6. What is the difference between *foundation cream* and cc cream?

7. List of best *foundation creams* for oily skin.
8. An ultimate guide for buying *foundation creams*.

You can check the previous chapter if you have a few more questions about creating a content calendar. I hope you got my drift.

Step 2: Keyword Research for Bloggers:

Even though we have learnt keyword research in the previous chapter, this is a summary. I included keyword research in writing a blog post because you know what is most searched in your niche.

When you understand the keyword research process and do it for every blog post you write, your probability of reaching an audience is higher.

This will help you find topics readers will want to read more about.

You have a gist of free paid SEO tools for keyword research.

I cover the quick winning tips in this post to get started with keyword research.

Step 1: Go to <u>Google keyword planner</u>– Click on Discover new keywords and enter the list of keywords you have chosen in the previous chapter.

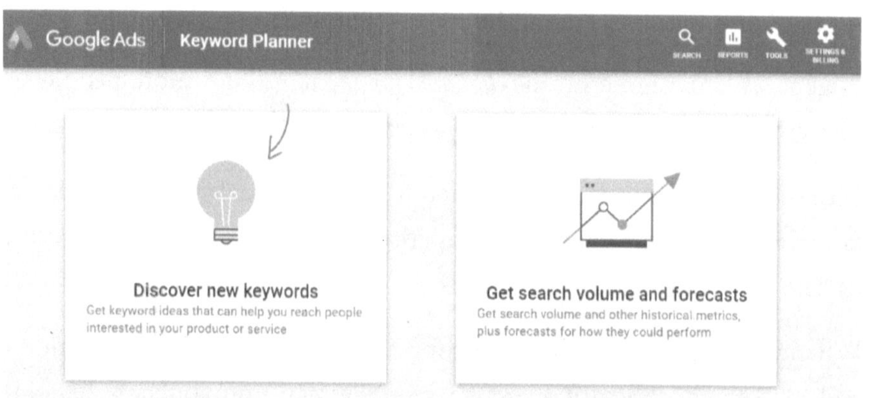

Step 2: Export them to a CSV file, open them, and find the keywords you can target.

Now the questions arise, how can I determine the best keywords for my blog post,

It requires the process of understanding two basic metrics in keyword research

- Search volume
- Search Difficulty

Search volume refers to how often a term(keyword) gets searched on Google.

Search Difficulty measures how hard it is to rank a keyword.

The below image shows you the output of Ubersuggest for detailed keyword research.

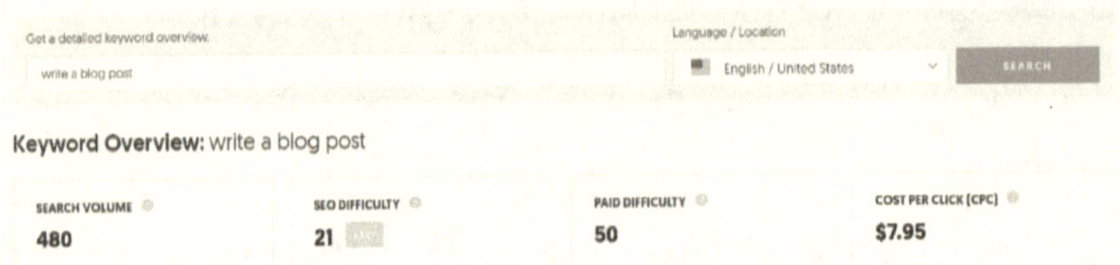

A quick and winning rule in keyword research:

Higher search volume means *demand for the topic*, and more people are interested in it. You have a *better opportunity to drive traffic.*

If the search difficulty is higher, then it is hard to rank for the particular keyword(which means more competitors are ranking, and you need a decent number of backlinks to rank for)

When you start, always try ranking for keywords with high search volume and low search difficulty. Here is where you can find your low-hanging fruit.

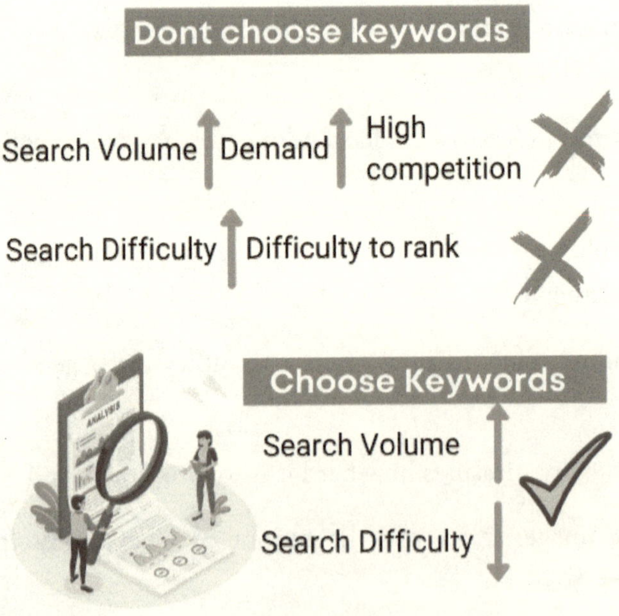

Step 3: Write your blog post outline:

Every blog post is like framing a story. A story needs a start and a finish with a compelling message in the middle. So now it's time to consolidate what you will share in the blog post.

Outlines help you cover every detail you wish to hide in the blog post while ensuring you are covering only a little. Without the outlines, you will miss the destination.

You might lose your time in unnecessary sections

Outlines can be like a gist encompassing the content you want to share.

It can be like this structure below, wherein you write the main heading and, with every main title, the concept you want to cover in a few points.

How to write a blog post in 2021 that captures audience attention

- Introduction
- Elements a perfect blog post
- Get to know your audience
- What is the end goal writing a blog post?
- 9 Step process for writing a blog post
- Step 1: Preparing your content calendar
- Step 2: Keyword research for blog posts
- Step 3: Preparing an Outline for your blog posts
- Step 4: A headline that grabs the readers attention
- Step 5: Writing Introduction that hooks the readers
- Step 6: Tell them a enchanting story
- Step 7: Crafty closure
- Step 8: Adding images to your blog post
- Step 9: Editing your blog posts like a pro
- How do you write a blog post?

So that you know what you want to cover in every section.

By now, you have created the basic structure of the blog post, and now it's time to detail every part of the blog post. Let's discuss how you can write every element of a blog post.

Step 4: writing an attention-grabbing headline:

Every headline's goal is to grab the scrollers' attention, stop them scrolling, and make them click and read your post.

The headline should capture the intention of your readers and powerfully communicate the essence of your blog post.

With the importance of headlines said, you understand the essence of writing headlines that increase the CTR(click-through rate). As you learn to write a blog post, write a quick headline and start writing your blog post. Later, you can finalize the headlines after writing the blog post.

"Spending too much time on writing headlines with all the tools without writing the content is like killing yourself."

Before I share writing headlines, I request you to write the headlines at the end of the blog post.

How to write attention-grabbing headlines for your blog post?

Before you begin, ask yourself these questions:

- Is your headline shareable? Does it have that curiosity factor that makes people shareable?
- Will it stand out in the noisy social world(I mean on Twitter and Facebook)
- Does your headline have powerful words or words that run in your reader's mind?

I always write my headlines at the end of the blog post. If I take 5 hours to complete the content, I will be exhausted. I write a simple working title and leave it overnight. The next day when I open for editing, I use the tools for analyzing the headlines and craft 3 to 4 working titles for my blog post.

Headline Formulas for your blog posts:

I'll showcase my readymade headline formulae and templates you can customize to write catchy and click-worthy titles. There are five formulas that I am going to address

1. How to headline:

How-to headlines are well-known and most used. These how-to headlines are the most famous because your readers have a problem to which you hold an answer. The success of this headline lies in the quality of your content. The way you solve a specific problem of your reader in-depth.

Example:

- *How to start a blog and make money online*
- *How to lose 5kgs a week without fat burners*
- *How to overcome failure and depression the better way.*

When looking at the above examples, I finish the headlines with a time frame or a pressing problem. Which means I am addressing a specific audience.

- *How to lose weight using the keto diet?*
- *How to make a choco vanilla cake without eggs.*

The more specific your headline is higher is your click-through rate.

2. The List headline:

Listicles are crowd-pleasing. Who doesn't love the long list of tips and tricks or hacks? A list post shares steps, hacks, tips, and tricks that lead the audience to the desired outcomes.

Examples:

- *7 Ways to grow your blog post with Pinterest*
- *101 Ways to persuade your readers with your words*

- *35 tips to make yourself sleep better*
- *3 successful ways to build traffic to your new blog.*

3. Comparison headline:

There are a lot of products available nowadays. People are information overloaded. Your readers are constantly looking for better reviews and opinions for the products they will buy. These comparison blog posts will give your readers the knowledge to decide.

Example:

- *Instagram vs Snapchat- Which social media platform to focus on for Gen Z*
- *Tik Tok vs Instagram Reels – What is better from the marketing standpoint?*
- Keto vs Paleo diet – Which is better for who?
- Lakme vs Loreal Kajal sticks – A comparison between the best.

4. Ultimate Guides headline:

Guides can be similar to "how to tutorial" posts. They teach the reader in an in-depth way. Sometimes it doesn't mean that way.

Examples:

- *An ultimate guide to using headline studio by coschedule headline analyzer*
- *The only guide you ever need to build a successful blog from scratch*
- *An Epic Guide on various methods of weight loss*

5. Results revealing headlines:

You are intimidating your readers with these headlines. You share the result directly in the headlines to make the readers click the blog post.

Example:

- *Get 10000 Instagram followers in just 6 months with this simple technique.*
- *Lose 5kgs a week with the keto diet.*

- *Lose your wrinkles in 5 weeks. That makes you look 5 years younger.*

Actionable tips on writing headlines for your blog posts:

1. Don't use Passive voice when writing headlines. Make sure you are always writing in active-passive.(Don't use passive voice in blog post too)
2. It's your priority to ensure you provide the in-depth content you promise with your headline.
3. Your headline should reinforce what is in it for the reader.
4. Verify whether your headline is using the language of the reader. Refrain from using industry jargon words that lead them to clarity.
5. Your headlines should provoke emotion. May it be an urgency or strong inspiration.
6. Headlines should be a go-getter. You don't need much creativity in headlines. Instead, it should touch and make the readers feel it's written for them.
7. Include numbers in your headlines, as they are catchy.
8. Make proper use of adjectives.
9. Let it have a better call to action.
10. Use emotional and powerful words in your headlines.
11. Use proper length for the titles.
12. Create 2-3 working versions of the headline to find out what's working.

Readymade headline templates that you can use now:

Till now, you have seen the types of headlines and writing tips. Now it's time to assist you with the headline templates.

> Note:
>
> This is not a fixed template. I have shown this too can be done. You can rearrange it the way you want it.At times keywords and what you want to deliver will be the same. Don't scratch your head for the words. Make sure you promise something to your reader. Find out what's stopping them from what they want to achieve and add them.With keyword research, you have a list of primary and secondary keywords; use them wisely.

Template 1:

How to + Action + Adjective+Keyword+ subject(Promise)

Example:

- How to lose weight naturally without diet plans
- How to start a blog to make money online
- How to beat the Instagram algorithm and grow your influence.

Template 2:

Number + Noun +adjective+keyword +Promise

Example:

- 7 tips on engaging with your followers the easy way
- 11 simple hacks to rank your blog
- 4 exercises that help you naturally lose belly fat

In the above examples, you see, I didn't use the template the same way; I rearranged it the way I wanted. You can grasp the template and use it the way you want.

Template 3:

Noun+Guide to +Action+Keyword+Promise

Example:

- An ultimate guide to using google keyword planner to find better keywords.
- The definitive guide to boosting your Instagram followers
- Easy guide on choosing the right foundation cream for your skin.

Template 4:

Emotional Word/Promise + Number +keyword +subject
Example:

- Top 20 bloggers sharing their best blogging tips
- Free tools to write better and faster.
- Stop doing these 12 things to grow your youtube subscribers.

Template 5:

Call to action+Keyword+Promise

Example:

- Signup now to receive your free resources to grow your blog
- Try these 20 tips to boost your blog traffic.

Here is a list of tools you can use to write captivating headlines for your blog post:

1. Coschedule's headline studio and the chrome extension.
2. Portent's title generator.

Step 5: Writing an introduction that hooks your readers:

After clicking on the title, what is the one sentence that will lead them to read the entire blog post?

Ask yourself the above question.

This is the importance of an introduction. Your blog post introduction is the first impression that says the gist of your content.

People don't read every blog post. They scan and scroll through your content. In the introduction, you have to say what is in the blog post.

As you are learning to write a blog post, here are a few dos and don't to write an introduction.

Try doing these things:

- Try different types of hooks in the starting paragraphs
- Use statistics or numbers that make them understand the importance of the context.
- Start with a story that unleashes something at the end
- Begin with a quote.
- Show them the result initially and reveal the path of the work later on in your blog post.

Don'ts:

- Bland, dull opening with hard-to-read sentences.
- Avoid cliches that keep them rolling their eyes.
- Too many repeated words and long sentences are very sticky, and readers feel the post is annoying.

The attention span of people is decreasing day by day. Instead of trying to clickbait your readers, try not to persuade them with no value.

To establish a connection with your readers, provide them with the important reasons to read the post to make them read the post and share it with their friends.

Step 6: Tell them an enchanting story:

People are returning to your blog to be entertained or learn something valuable.

Imagine yourself as a dull teacher who teaches only the context. What is the use of teaching? As a teacher or a mentor, your work should enhance and uplifts your students' lives. How can you encourage someone with just a text? You need emotions to convey to the reader that brings life to the context.

The same is true here; you can portray the information like a newspaper. Think about how you can make a difference in your writing to glitter like a bar of gold.

The same information in an article can be better conveyed as a story that travels with the readers.

How can you portray the information in a story?

<u>Answer the most asked questions in the community</u>: One of the most important things you should include in your content is your community's most asked questions. To find the most asked questions, Type in your query in google, see the relevant questions for your blog post and address them in one of your subheadings.

<u>Include the lessons from your learnings</u>: Instead of simply asking the readers to do things, including your studies, like how you did and how to do. Cover every roadblock you face and show them how they can overcome it.

<u>Use visuals wherever needed</u>: Images convey better than the text. Use screenshots or images of the process.

Here are a few tips that will help you develop a better copy.

- Write for Readers First- use "you" instead of mentioning "reader."

- Organize your sales messages inside the copy. Let them be hidden behind the information you are sharing.
- Make sure to use shorter paragraphs. Check the readability of the blog posts in the Hemingway app.
- Neil Patel recommends using one-sentence paragraphs, which are accessible for the readers to consume.
- Write in a conversational style.
- Make bullet points and lists when and wherever required

I usually write the main theme headings in the outline. So, while coming to the writing process, I need to fill in the context for the particular paragraphs. I suggest you spend some more time outlining your blog post. That is an excellent time-saving tip.

Now that with an idea of what to cover in your blog post. When you address your readers personally with a personal touch everywhere, the blog post feels personal.

The best thing you can do to build a business blogging is to learn how to write a blog post. Many courses are available, but the most valuable lessons are learnt by writing and practising them daily.

Step 7: Write a crafty Closure:

Like the opening statements, the closing triggers are the most important.

You have written a headline with a great headline score, and your headline is persuading me to click. Following the headline, you write an introduction that flows nicely, and the content is heavy and powerful with loads of information.

Now just a few final lines to write and end your blog post. What to do and what to write?

Your final lines are the final gist, and they must make your readers take the desired action you want to.

Now, we will see how to make them act without asking them to.

What makes closing paragraphs so emotional and inspirational?

Most bloggers don't write a heart-warming final paragraph. They share tips, tutorials, or ideas; that's it. They finish their blog post.

Think of this for a second, as a blogger, is simply sharing the tips your task?

My answer is undoubtedly NO.

Every blogger has to encourage the readers, make them feel good, initiate an action… to be a good mentor.

How do mentors inspire people?

Start with asking or imagining your ideal reader. Try finding answers to these questions

- *What is stopping them from executing your tips/advice?*
- *Did your reader feel overwhelmed at the end of the blog post?*
- *Did they think they could not do or achieve it?*
- *Did he think it was too much effort for a bit of gain?*

When you understand your favourite reader, you can help him with specific, actionable advice at the end of the blog post. Give a trumpet call that flourishes them with the benefits of implementing your advice.

What could be the aim of your final paragraph?

It could be something like

Asking them to pin your infographics

Share your blog post

Sign up for your Email newsletter

Buy your product

Take your service

Buy your affiliate product

Sign up for your webinar or course.

Once you have identified your final paragraph's aim, write a plain draft and edit it with powerful words that invigorate your readers.

Step 8: Adding visuals to your blog post:

Now you are about to finish learning to write a blog post. It is an image to emphasize in a blog post and its importance and how you can do it.

The human brain deciphers visuals much quicker than text. The text takes a long and linear time to decode.

Most content marketers here use images in their blog posts that summarise or portray the essence of their content.

What is the purpose of an image in a blog post?

Like how you cannot bake bread and add an image of a cake, the same way you cannot share any image you want to upload. The picture you are sharing must be relevant to the message of your story.

I read articles from top blogs every day. Sometimes I read lengthy blog posts to understand the writer's mind—his way of conveying the content.

The visuals that appear in the blog posts have a specific goal.

The goals of an Image can be

- To explain a process[How you can do]
- To emphasize an important point[Stats, tips]
- Showcase their personality[Infographics]
- Build a brand experience[using storytelling arts]

Step 9: SEO your blog posts:

Once you finish editing and adding images, it's time to optimize your writing for the search engines. There are several things you can do instantly. Even if you are not an SEO expert, You can use these simple tips to ensure you have done what is needed.

It would help if you had a keyword-targeting structure.

Let's see that.

Keyword Research for Targeting structure for On-page SEO

Just because your headline score is 90 doesn't mean you will rank No 1 in google. Your content quality plays a vital role in organizing your posts.

Use primary keyword in Title: Use the primary keyword in the title and URL.

Use the primary keyword in the first paragraph: Place your primary keyword in the first sentence. But sometimes, when you have to convey an interesting story or a hook in the introduction, you can skip this.

Spread your secondary keyword in your content: Naturally, add the secondary and LSI keywords to your blog post. This is how you can rank your post for multiple keywords. Use the secondary keyword in one of your subheadings.

Use Internal links: Link your old blog posts related to the post.

Use keywords in Metadata: Think meta description as your sales copy. If you have written a 5000 words long blog post, you must convince your readers and Bots in 2-3 lines. That is the meta description. Don't forget to include keywords in the metadata.

Optimize your URL: If you use an SEO plugin like Yoast or Rank Math, You can optimize your URL in the plugin. I mean the Permalink. Or else you can optimize your Permalink in the WordPress setup menu.

Format and use alt tags in images: Use the best images with small file sizes and add keywords in the photos' alt text. You can rank for the keywords in the image search too.

Write for Humans, not for Bots: After reading this, you may have to write with keywords in mind. You cannot create content if you are thinking about SEO. You can write only if you think of your reader in your mind.

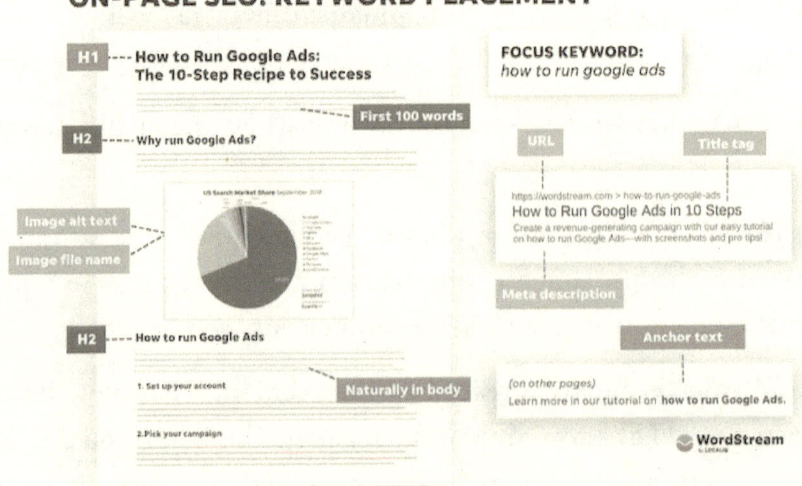

Action Steps:

1. Start writing blog posts.
2. Write atleast 2 articles before you launch your blog.

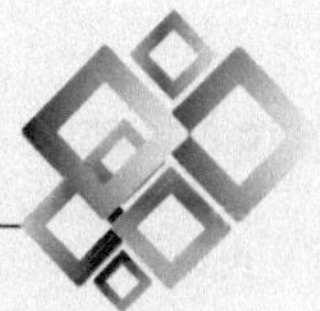

CHAPTER 8

TRAFFIC GENERATION

*I*magine pouring your heart and soul into crafting a beautifully written blog post.

You meticulously edit and optimize it for SEO, and finally, with trembling excitement, you hit the "publish" button.

You sit back and wait, eager to see the flood of traffic and engagement that will surely follow.

But instead, you're met with deafening silence.

Your post is lost in a sea of content buried beneath the endless stream of daily blog posts.

Your hard work goes unnoticed, leaving you feeling frustrated and disheartened.

But there's no need to despair.

With the right strategies and tools, you can rise above the noise and attract the audience your content deserves

In this chapter, we'll dive into the different channels of growth and how you can strategically choose the right one to promote your blog post.

Where do people go wrong? Why do some excellent blog posts go unheard?

There are two critical aspects of running a successful blog:

1. Creating incredible content
2. Distributing the content well

As we have seen in the previous chapters, creating incredible content is just one piece of the puzzle. The other vital piece is distributing that content effectively. Unfortunately, most writers focus only on creating content and neglect the distribution aspect, leading to mediocre results.

It's essential to strike a balance between content creation and distribution. Imagine the content you create is like a rocket you build, and content distribution is like launching that rocket into space. Your rocket and content will never leave the ground without a proper launch plan. Content distribution is the key to propelling your content into the world, and reaching new heights and audiences.

The writing-to-distribution ratio is a crucial piece of the puzzle for running a successful blog. It should be 50:50, meaning you spend equal amounts of time writing great content and promoting it to the world.

Imagine pouring your heart and soul into creating a piece of content, only to have it sit on your blog without any visitors. It's like baking a delicious cake and leaving it to rot in the pantry. To avoid this, you need to devote just as much time to promoting your content as you do to creating it.

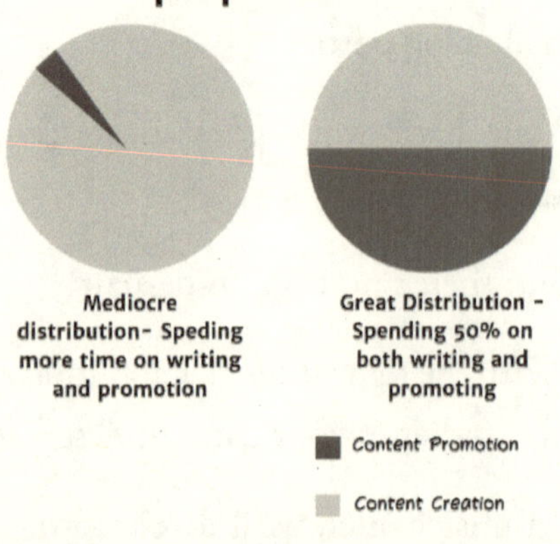

Instead of churning out ten mediocre articles that go unnoticed, focus on creating one exceptional piece of content and promoting it relentlessly. This strategy may take more time and effort upfront, but the results will be worth it.

A top 1% article has the potential to be shared 1000 times, reaching an audience far beyond what you could achieve with ten mediocre pieces of content.

So, do whatever it takes to bring your articles into that top 1%. Invest the time and resources needed to create truly remarkable content, and then dedicate equal effort to promoting it using every distribution channel available to you.

By striking a balance between content creation and distribution, you can launch your content like a rocket ship into the stratosphere and reach new heights of success.

"Unleashing the Science behind Viral Content: How to Create Shareable Blog Posts"

Have you ever felt the thrill of seeing someone sharing a screenshot of their blog post traffic?

Or the excitement of tweets about getting 10k readers for a blog post on the day of publishing?

It's like a rush of adrenaline that comes with achieving a significant milestone in your blogging journey.

Every content creator's dream is to write a blog post that becomes wildly popular and spreads across the internet like wildfire. But what makes specific blog posts go viral while others go unnoticed?

To understand the science behind viral blog posts, we need to delve into the concept of traffic.

Traffic refers to the number of visitors or clicks on a website or piece of content. The more traffic a blog post gets, the more likely it is to be shared and spread to a broader audience.

So, what exactly is viral content? It's an article that generates high engagement(Likes, shares, etc.) and is rapidly shared across various online platforms, such as social media, blogs, and forums. Viral blog posts can take many forms, including listicles, how-to guides, opinion pieces, and case studies.

But why do specific blog posts go viral while others do not? The answer lies in a few factors that contribute to the success of viral blog posts:

- Viral blog posts often have an emotional appeal and elicit a strong reaction from readers, whether amusement, anger, or inspiration.
- They are highly shareable and easily digestible, with catchy headlines, attention-grabbing visuals, and concise writing that speaks to the reader's senses.
- Viral content taps into a trending topic or current event, making them highly relevant and timely.

In summary, creating viral blog posts is the ultimate goal for every content creator. It's a pursuit that requires profoundly understanding your audience, tapping into their emotions, and committing to creating highly shareable and relevant content. By leveraging the science behind viral content, you can increase your chances of making blog posts that resonate with your audience and generate significant traffic to your website.

Why do People Share Content?

In today's digital age, sharing content has become an integral part of our online lives. We share everything from photos and videos to articles and blog posts. But have you ever wondered why we feel compelled to share content in the first place?

Understanding why people share content is crucial for content creators looking to create highly shareable content that resonates with their audience. By tapping into the motivations behind content sharing, we can create content that connects with our readers on a deeper level, encouraging them to share it with their network.

There are several reasons why people share content:

1. **To connect with others:** Sharing content is a way to start a conversation with others, to let them know what we're interested in, and to find like-minded people.78% of people share content to stay connected with people they may not otherwise stay in touch with. (New York Times)

2. **To show our personality:** By sharing content, we can express our personality and values, and show others what we stand for.

3. **To provide value:** People share content that they find useful or informative, with the goal of helping others.

4. **To entertain:** Let's face it, sometimes we share content just because it's funny, heartwarming, or entertaining.

5. **To establish expertise:** Sharing content can also be a way to establish ourselves as experts in our field, whether it's through sharing industry news, research, or insights. According to the <u>Newyork Times study</u>, 49% of respondents share as it allows them to inform others of products they care about and potentially change opinions or encourage actions.

6. **To stay top of mind:** By consistently sharing content, we can stay top of mind with our followers and maintain a presence in their feeds.

Understanding why people share content is crucial for content creators and marketers. Creating content that aligns with these motivations can increase the chances of your content being shared and reaching a broader audience.

The Channels of Growth

We now know why people share content, but how can we ensure our content gets in front of those potential sharers?

Content distribution channels refer to the different platforms and methods to share your content with your intended audience, such as social media, email, search engines, and more. By understanding and utilizing different distribution channels, you can maximize the visibility and impact of your content. To drive traffic, you should share your content strategically.

The channels can be divided into three distinct categories:

1. **Owned channels** are your own and control distribution channels, such as your website, blog, and your email list. You can promote your content on these channels by optimizing for search engines, sharing on social media, and delivering email newsletters to your subscribers.

2. **Earned or shared channels** – These are the channels where you leverage other people's audiences to promote your content. This can include mentions and shares from other creators on social media, reviews written by others, or brand mentions by others.

3. **Paid channels** – This category includes any promotion methods that require a financial investment, such as paid social media advertising, sponsored content, or newsletter sponsorships.

Content Distribution Channels

Owned Channels	Earned Channels	Paid Channels
Your Blog	Brand mentions	Pay-per-click campaigns
Email newsletters	Guest Posts	Social media ads
Your social profiles	Press Release	Sponsorships

Paid channels usually yield quicker results, but they require an initial investment. On the other hand, owned and earned channels are organic and often need more time to establish, but they offer greater sustainability and longevity.

Organic Traffic

Organic traffic refers to the visitors who visit your website through search engine results pages (SERPs) without any paid promotion. The previous chapter, Keyword Research, teaches you to write articles that rank on Google. Here are some tips to help you get organic traffic:

1. Research relevant keywords: Find out what keywords your target audience is searching for and incorporate them into your content to rank higher in SERPs. Using the method we learnt in the previous chapter.

2. Optimize your website: Make sure your website is optimized for search engines by using meta tags, meta descriptions, alt tags for images, and other on-page SEO techniques.

3. Create quality content: Produce high-quality content that is relevant, engaging, and informative for your target audience. This will increase the chances of your content being shared, linked to, and ultimately ranking higher in search results.

4. Use internal linking: Link to other relevant pages on your website within your content to help search engines understand your website's structure and improve visitors' navigation.

5. Build backlinks: Acquire quality backlinks from other websites to your website. This signals to search engines that your website is authoritative and trustworthy, which can increase your rankings.

6. Utilize social media: Share your content on social media platforms to increase its visibility and encourage social shares, which can help drive organic traffic.

7. Be patient: Organic traffic takes time, so be patient and consistent with your efforts. Keep producing quality content and optimizing your website for search engines; you will eventually see results.

As we have dedicated a chapter to driving organic traffic, we now continue with the other traffic generation tactics.

Email List Building:

Shivani Kapila, a Surat-based content creator, had left her job as an HR professional to pursue TikTok full-time. Even when the news of the TikTok ban was all over the internet, she was in complete disbelief. "It was really shocking to see the app go offline overnight. Panicked, I kept looking and refreshing my account. I could see all the hard work that got me 10 million followers going out of sight like it was never there. Shivani said that TikTok was the only social media platform she was active on. It took her a little over five months to deal with the damage created by TikTok's ban in India and get on to other platforms.

This real incident happened to many content <u>creators in India.</u> [31] If Shivani had an email list, she had some or the other way of communicating with her followers.

In a world where social media platforms are constantly changing their algorithms and policies, your email list is the one asset that you truly own.

It's like a piece of land that you can cultivate, develop and reap the rewards for years to come. It's a sensory experience that engages your audience with personalized messages and meaningful content.

Building an email list is not just about capturing email addresses; it's about building relationships and trust with your subscribers. This way, you can promote your content, products, and services to them directly without worrying about algorithm changes or platform restrictions.

How to build an email list?

Here are some steps to help you get started:

1. Define your goals: Before you start any email marketing campaign, you need to know what you want to achieve. Do you want to promote a new product or service, increase website traffic, or drive more sales? Once you have defined your goals, you can create a plan that aligns with them.

2. Choose an email marketing service: There are many email marketing services available, such as Mailerlite, Mailchimp, ConvertKit, or Constant Contact. Choose one that best suits your needs and budget.

3. Create a lead magnet: Offer something of value to your audience in exchange for their email address, such as an ebook, discount code, or exclusive content.

4. Add opt-in forms to your website: Opt-in forms can be added to your website, landing pages, or blog posts to encourage visitors to sign up for your email list.

5. Promote your lead magnet: Share your lead magnet on social media, guest blog posts, or other relevant platforms to drive traffic to your opt-in forms.

6. Provide valuable content: Consistently send valuable and relevant content to your subscribers to maintain their interest and trust.

7. Monitor your results: Monitor your email open rates, click-through rates, and other metrics to measure the success of your email campaigns and adjust your strategy as needed.

Remember to always prioritize the privacy and consent of your subscribers by following anti-spam laws and offering opt-out options in your emails.

Lead Magnets you can offer:

Lead magnets are the powerful tool that can attract potential customers to your website by offering them something valuable in exchange for their contact information. It's like a tempting aroma wafting from your kitchen, enticing your guests to come and taste what you're cooking.

A well-crafted lead magnet can provide immense value to your audience, making them eager to hand over their email address or other contact details. From ebooks and cheat sheets to webinars and exclusive access, the possibilities for lead magnets are endless. Invest in a compelling lead magnet that will leave them craving more of your offer.

Lead Magnet Ideas

Checklist	Resource List	Quiz	Gated Content
Cheatsheet	Calendar	Survey	Tutorial
Template	Plan/Planner Worksheet/	Giveaway	eBook
Swipe File	Workbook	Manifesto	Guide
Examples	Printable	Comic Strip	Report
Script	Inspiration File	Quotes	Infographic
Toolkit	Prompts	Mobile App/Game	Webinar
Web App	Spreadsheet	Event Tickets	
	Recipes	Email Course	
		Free Coaching Session	

<u>Tools to help you create popups:</u>

1. **Elementor Popup Builder:** This is a built-in feature of Elementor that allows you to create different types of popups, such as lightbox, fullscreen, slide-in, and more. You can customize your popups using the drag-and-drop interface of Elementor and choose from various triggers and conditions to display your popups.

2. **Popup Maker:** This free WordPress plugin allows you to create customizable popups using Elementor. You can choose from various templates and customize them to match your brand. Popup Maker also offers a variety of triggers and conditions to display your popups.

3. **OptinMonster** - a popular and user-friendly tool that allows you to create various types of popups and opt-in forms.

4. **Sumo** - a free tool that offers multiple features, including popups, welcome mats, and scroll-triggered boxes.

5. Thrive Leads - a plugin that provides a wide range of customizable opt-in forms, including popups, slide-ins, and sticky ribbons.

Methods to build an email list:

As mentioned above, your lead magnet is ready and signed for the email service provider. You can add signup forms and popup forms to your website.

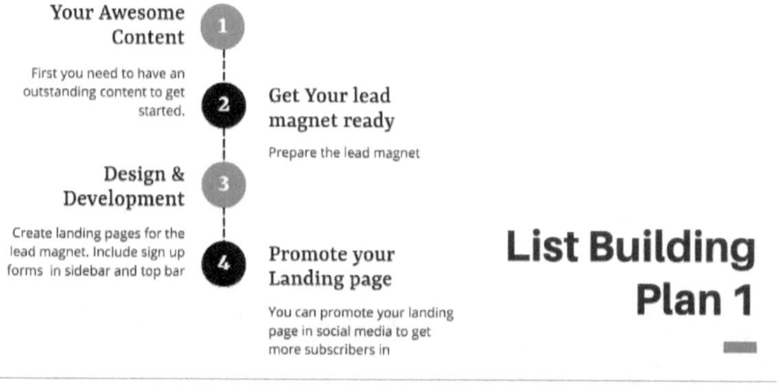

An example signup form:
Offering an eBook:

Step 1: Add a relevant CTA to your Blog post.

Ex: If your Blog post is *"25 List-building tactics every blogger should know."* *Then your lead magnet may be a lead magnet checklist or an Ebook.*

Step 2: Create a Popup or add your list-building form from your email service.

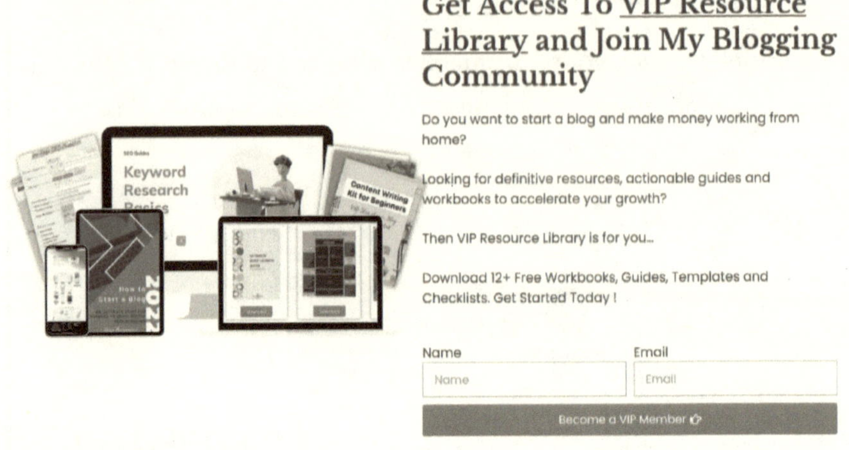

Step 3: Create a separate landing page like mine to build your email list. <u>You can become a member by clicking on this link</u> or https://durgathiyagarajan.in/blogging-resource-library/.

The overall process looks like this:

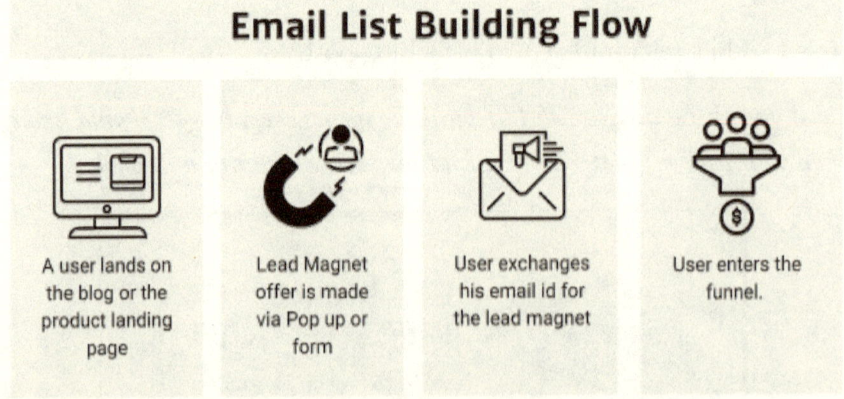

Popup placement ideas:

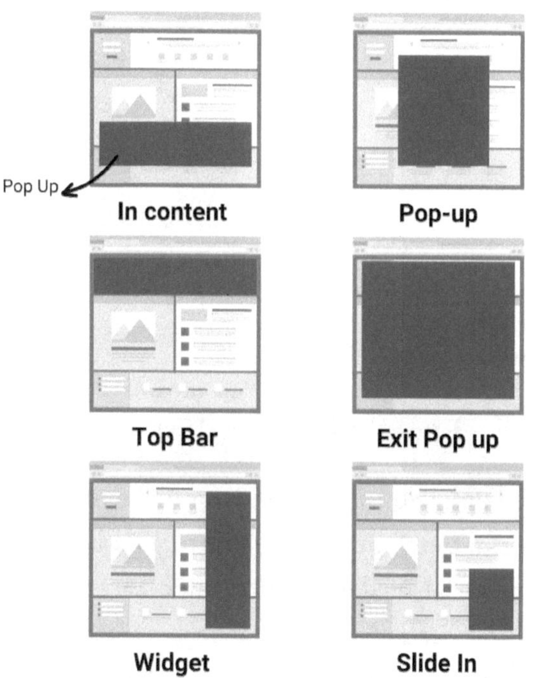

POPULAR POP-UP PLACEMENT

Email your list:

We covered the process of building your email list. Now it's time to leverage it. Sending an email to your list of subscribers is a powerful way to drive traffic to your latest blog post. But don't stop there. Encourage your subscribers to engage with your content by commenting, liking, and sharing it with their community. This will help you reach a larger audience. Since your subscribers have already shown an interest in your content by signing up for your email list, they are more likely to share it with their followers.

You can include the link to your latest blog posts in the email signature.

<u>Wisestamp</u> and <u>Hubspot</u> email generator helps you with this. Just like the button in the image below, that takes readers to the blog.

CHRISTINE HOUSE

Inerrior Design Blogger **House Design**

202-556-8896   christine@housedesign.com
www.housedesign.com

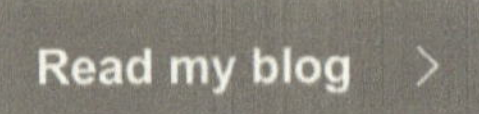

Read my blog >

Social Media Traffic:

In today's fast-paced online business world, it's no secret that social media has become a powerful tool for driving traffic to your blog. With millions of people active on social media platforms like Facebook, Twitter, and Instagram, it has become essential to leverage these platforms to reach your target audience and grow your online presence. Social media provides a direct line of communication between you and your audience, making it easier than ever to build relationships and establish trust with potential customers.

Getting traffic from Facebook:

As a blogger, you can't afford to overlook Facebook, which is undoubtedly the largest social media platform out there.

Whenever I publish an article on my website, I post it as a Facebook update. This approach helps me with five things,

1. Get instant traffic once the articles go live.
2. Get more comments from my audience.
3. Speed up the indexation of the newly published content.

4. Further, push me to make the post epic.
5. Make myself accountable to my audience.

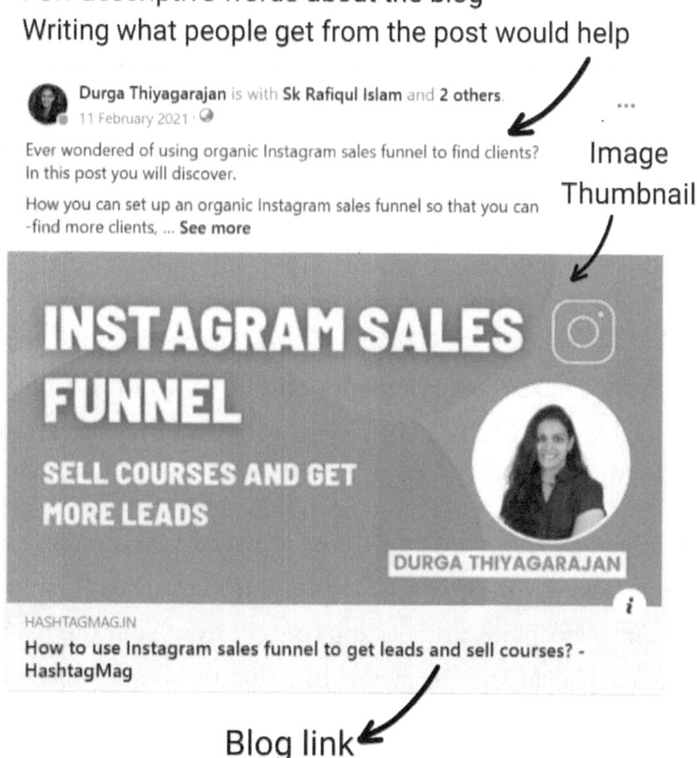

> <u>Tips:</u>
>
> - Before publishing your article, make a Facebook post that you will publish an article on the topic "XXXXX".
> - Create a nice and simple description of your post. You can use the headline templates shown in the previous chapter.

Ignite Your Blog's Potential with the Power of Twitter

Incorporating Twitter into your multichannel traffic acquisition strategy can greatly benefit your blog.

One of the best ways to leverage Twitter for blog traffic is to include click-to-tweet buttons on your blog posts. Tools like <u>Thrive Architect</u> and <u>Click to Tweet</u> can help you easily create content boxes that allow your readers to share your blog post with their Twitter followers.

Note: *You can repurpose the blog post to multiple tweet threads.*

Getting traffic from Quora:

If you're looking for long-term traffic for your blog, Quora is a platform you shouldn't overlook.

Why?

Because every time someone upvotes one of your answers on Quora, it becomes visible to all of that person's followers, which can result in a steady stream of traffic to your site.

So how do you go about writing Quora answers? One strategy that works well is repurposing your existing blog content. However, it's important to note that simply copying and pasting content from your blog onto Quora is considered plagiarism. To avoid this, slightly modify the text to suit Quora's audience and include a great introduction, formatting, images, and short paragraphs.

Using LinkedIn Traffic:

Optimize your blog post for LinkedIn: Make sure your blog post is optimized for LinkedIn by adding a meta description, a compelling headline, and a featured image relevant to your content.

Share your post on LinkedIn: Share your post as a status update or an article. When you share it as an article, LinkedIn will show it to more people and be more visible in search results.

Use relevant hashtags: Use relevant hashtags in your post to make it more discoverable. You can use up to three hashtags per post. Make sure the hashtags you use are relevant to your content.

Engage with your audience: Engage with your audience by responding to comments, thanking people for sharing your post, and sharing your post with your network. This will help you build a community around your content.

Note: Instead of copying and pasting the entire blog post, you can write a compelling copy and include read more, which can take people to the LinkedIn article.

Visual Platforms:
Pin it on Pinterest.

If you're blogging about recipes, DIY stuff, or anything that can be conveyed better with visual content, you can't ignore Pinterest. It's the go-to platform for bloggers, marketers, and businesses who want to showcase their visual content and get more eyes on their work.

To make the most of Pinterest, you need to create custom visuals that are both engaging and informative. And the good news is that you don't need to be a graphic designer or spend a lot of money to create them.

Plenty of online tools like Canva and Piktochart are easy to use and free. With these tools, you can create stunning visuals in no time and make your content stand out on Pinterest.

Note: *You can download my Pinterest Algorithm Guide from the Resource Library. That has every pinch of detail nailed down to play with pins.*

Grow with the Gram:

At first, Instagram had no option for sharing links. This was a massive disadvantage for bloggers. Now Instagram is more than a visual platform for sharing photos. You can create reels(short videos), Stories, Guides, Carousels, and Standalone images.

You cannot directly add your blog posts. Instead, you can repurpose them into images. I use Instagram to grow my business.

If you have a Canva Pro account, You can turn one blog post into three carousels and more. If you are interested in videos, you can create reels or long-form portrait videos too.

Note: Download Instagram Algorithm Guide from Resource Library to use the platform. If you are interested in Video creation, you can repurpose your blog into a Youtube video.

Community chats and Niche-Forums:

Engage on Reddit:

Reddit can be tricky to master, especially since users quickly spot overly self-promotional posts, and they may downvote them. However, you can still successfully drive traffic to your blog from the platform if you are careful and tasteful. Focusing on connecting with the community and building relationships with dedicated commenters is essential. Once you have established a good reputation, you can start making posts asking for your content's feedback.

Note:

1. *Use the Sub Reddit tool we used in Chapter 2 to find your niche and your subreddit.*
2. *Engage with people and upvote others' opinions.*
3. *Make friends and build a relationship with other Redditors.*

Once in a while, promoting your post may not seem spammy. You can use the same strategy for Facebook groups.

Niche Forums:

Google Search: Start with a basic search of your niche keywords and the word "forum" or "community". For example, if you are in the fitness niche, you can search "fitness forums" or "fitness communities".

Here are some examples of search operators you can use on Google to find niche forums and communities:

1. [your niche] + "forum"
2. [your niche] + "community"
3. [your niche] + "discussion board"
4. [your niche] + "message board"
5. [your niche] + "group"
6. [your niche] + "chat"

Remember, once you have found niche forums and communities, engaging with the members and providing value to the community before promoting your content is essential. Building a reputation and rapport with the community will make driving traffic to your blog easier in the long run.

In summary, you must be an active and engaged online community member to drive social media traffic to your blog. Building relationships with your followers and providing valuable content can establish trust and credibility, leading to increased traffic and engagement.

Guest Blogging:

Guest blogging is a widespread technique where bloggers write articles for other websites within the same niche or industry. By collaborating with other websites, bloggers can get their content in front of new readers, build relationships with other bloggers and their communities, and increase their visibility on search engines.

REGULAR **BLOG POSTING**

GUEST **BLOG POSTING**

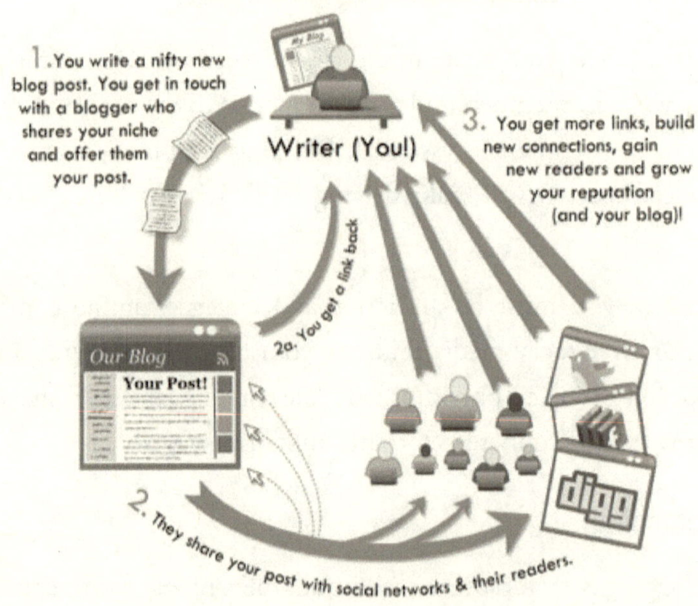

This "Guest Infographic" was created by Brandon Rhodes through MyBlogGuest

How does it work?

You write a blog post for another website in your niche, and you get to include a link back to your website in exchange. This link is called a backlink, and the more high-quality backlinks your website has, the higher it will rank in search results.

But it's not just about getting backlinks. Guest blogging also helps you build relationships with other bloggers and website owners in your niche. By guest blogging on their websites and building a rapport with them, you become part of a community of like-minded individuals. This community can help you promote your content and drive more traffic to your website, making it an essential part of any blogger's strategy.

So, if you want to build your website's authority, increase its visibility, and become part of a community of bloggers and website owners in your niche, start guest blogging today!

How to find guest-posting blogs?

Pre-Preparation

To kick-start your guest blogging journey, it's crucial to understand the value you bring to the table. Please think about what you can gain from it, but focus on what benefits you can offer the site you want to contribute.

To begin, ask yourself

1. what value you can provide.
2. Does your expertise align with the audience's interests?
3. Does your writing style match what the blog's readers are looking for?
4. Can you assist in filling their editorial calendar with content?
5. Are you capable of building quality backlinks through your guest posts?

Understanding your worth will help you identify suitable opportunities and create a more compelling outreach strategy. By offering genuine value to the blog, you increase your chances of securing a guest blogging spot and building lasting relationships with fellow bloggers.

First, your initial task is to locate a website accepting guest posts.

There are two possible ways; You can use Google search or paid SEO tools. Let's start with Google search operators. You have the Guest Blogging Blueprint sheet free with this book; download it and do it with me. Record all the blogs you find. So that you have a repository for blogs you can pitch.

HOW TO GUEST BLOG

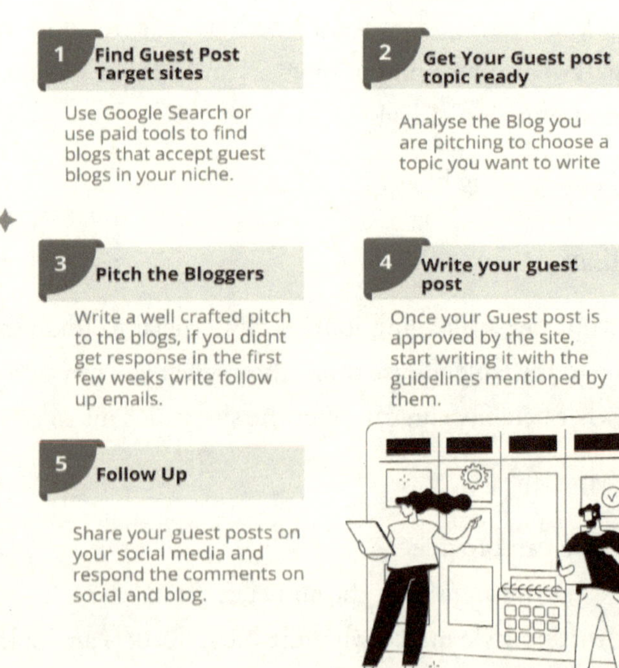

Step 1: Find Guest Posting Opportunities:

Once you have the Guest Blogging Excel sheet ready to store data, it's time to explore guest blogging opportunities on websites within your niche.

Depending on the level of your blog, you can either broaden your search to include a wider range of websites or focus solely on your target audience. However, remember that a backlink from a relevant website holds more significance than one from an irrelevant site.

Here are some search strings that can help you find guest posting opportunities on Google:

- "write for us" + [your niche]
- "submit a guest post" + [your niche]
- "guest post by" + [your niche]
- "guest post guidelines" + [your niche]
- "guest post opportunities" + [your niche]
- "guest post submission" + [your niche]
- "contribute to our site" + [your niche]
- "become a guest blogger" + [your niche]
- "guest author" + [your niche]
- "looking for guest posts" + [your niche]
- "accepting guest posts" + [your niche]
- "write for our blog" + [your niche]
- Your Keyword "submit an article"
- Your Keyword "submit article"
- Your Keyword "guest author"
- Your Keyword "send a tip"
- Your Keyword inurl: "guest blogger"
- Your Keyword inurl: "guest post"
- allintitle: Your Keyword + guest post
- Your Keyword "writers wanted"
- Your Keyword "articles wanted"
- Your Keyword "become an author"
- Your Keyword "become guest writer"
- Your Keyword "become a contributor."

Alternatively, You can use Twitter to find Guest Blog opportunities. Head over to Twitter, search and try the string

Your Keyword +Guest Blog

Here's the blog I got from the search.

Use Paid tools:

I use Uber suggest, but you can try tools like Ahrefs, Semrush etc. Uber Suggest is beginner friendly.

- Add your competitor's home page link in the backlinks overview section.
- Download the backlinks.csv from Uber Suggest and analyze the links to find where they have written guest posts. Not all the backlinks are from guest posts. You have to mine deeper and filter the sites.

Step 2: Find the Perfect Guest Post Topic:

Once you have the master file of the list of blogs accepting guest posts ready, examine every blog to find the topic you want to write.

- Pick a site and look at the most popular posts on the site. You can usually find them listed in the blog's sidebar. Analyze what type of content they write and What would be the correct pitch you can do.
- Use Hunter.io to find the email id of the blogger if there is no form to submit a guest blog pitch.
- Alternatively, On Uber Suggest finding their top-performing pages to get an idea of what type of content resonates well with their audience.

Step 3: Send your pitch

Sending a generic pitch to every outlet is a surefire way to get your guest post rejected. Editors from prominent publications receive hundreds of pitches every week. You must personalize your pitch to each outlet to avoid being deleted immediately.

Here are some things to keep in mind while preparing your pitch:

- Carefully reading and adhering to the submission instructions is crucial. Failure to do so may give the impression to the editor that you are not entirely dedicated to the opportunity. This entails following the required format and avoiding proposing topics they have explicitly stated as unacceptable.
- Before pitching any articles, checking the publisher's previously published content is best. If they've already covered the topic you had in mind, it's best to avoid pitching it. You can use the Google search feature **site:website.com** to confirm.
- Please provide samples of your work, such as links to 2-3 relevant articles you have previously published.
- If their guidelines allow it, presenting various topics will allow them to choose the option that best suits their needs.

- When submitting pitches, please provide a brief description of each topic. Keep it to 1-2 sentences at most. This will help the editor better understand the potential of your pitch, especially if the title is not descriptive enough and reads like clickbait.
- When reaching out, it's best to keep your introduction brief but informative. Start by introducing yourself and stating the purpose of your message.

Here's the email template I use,

Dear [Editor's Name],

My name is [Your Name], and I am a [Your Position/Title] at [Your Company/Blog].

I recently discovered [Publication Name] and was impressed by the quality of content on your website.

I hope to contribute to your website and submit a guest post for your consideration.

Here are a few ideas that I think your readers would be interested in:

[Topic Idea #1]: [Brief Description of Topic Idea #1]

[Topic Idea #2]: [Brief Description of Topic Idea #2]

[Topic Idea #3]: [Brief Description of Topic Idea #3]

If any of these ideas interest you, please let me know, and I can provide a more detailed outline. I have attached links to some of the previously published work that would be relevant to your audience.

[Link to Work Sample #1]

[Link to Work Sample #2]

Thank you for considering my guest post. I look forward to hearing from you soon.

Best regards,

[Your Name]

Step 4: Follow-Up Email:

Most guest post pitches do not get a response, so be encouraged if you are still waiting to hear back from all of the 50 guest post pitches you sent. While some editors may not respond because they are uninterested, others may need to remember. Therefore, sending a follow-up email is always a good idea unless stated otherwise on their website.

For small publications, waiting at least two weeks before sending a follow-up email is best. For more prominent publications, it's better to wait between three and four weeks. If they still do not respond to your follow-up email, it's best to leave them alone. You want to be remembered as something other than the annoying marketer who would not stop spamming them.

Also, it's common to receive a reply several months later. Sometimes the timing might need to be corrected, or the topic might not be a good fit at that moment. But don't worry; it's okay. Just keep pitching, and you'll eventually find the right fit.

Here's the follow-up email template:

> *Hello [Editor's Name],*
>
> *I hope this email finds you well. I recently sent over a guest post pitch for [Publication Name] and wanted to follow up to see if you had a chance to review it.*
>
> *If you have any inquiries, feel free to ask me. I appreciate your time and consideration.*
>
> *Best regards, [Your Name]*

Step 5: write your Guest Post:

Bringing your best work forward is essential to ensure that your guest post gets published and makes a positive impact. Here are the critical ingredients for a successful guest post:

- Follow the guidelines.
- Replicate the style: Read their previous blog posts to understand their tone, style, and formatting. By matching their writing style, your post will require less editing, and the editor will be more likely to publish it.
- Include internal links: Incorporating internal links to their website shows that you have researched their content and are interested in building a relationship with them.
- Relevant external links: Include links that provide additional value to readers and relate to your topic. Avoid spammy or irrelevant links, which can hurt your credibility.
- Check grammar and spelling: Typos and grammatical errors can detract from the quality of your writing and decrease the chances of acceptance. Use free tools like Grammarly and Hemingway App to proofread your work.
- Add images: Include relevant and high-quality images to make your post visually appealing and enhance its quality. Avoid generic stock images and instead use your unique images or screenshots.

Step 6: Share your Guest Post:

Once your guest post is published, thank the editor and here are the two things you should do without fail.

1. Actively respond to the comments you receive on the post.
2. Share your guest post on social media. If the editor shares on their social media page, thank them and comment on the post.

> Note:
>
> I have mentioned easy ways of driving traffic to the new sites. You have a lot many options like content syndication and repurposing. For the sake of simplicity, I didn't include those things here.

Paid Advertising:

Paid advertising can be an effective way to drive traffic to your blog. Here are some steps you can take:

1. Define your audience: Determine your target audience and what interests them. This will help you choose the right advertising platforms and create effective ads. Here's a sample audience set I use for the Facebook ads:

Demographics:

- Age: 18-45
- Gender: All
- Location: United States
- Language: English

1. Interests:

- Blogging
- Content creation
- Writing
- Social media
- SEO
- Entrepreneurship
- Digital Marketing
- Online business
- Personal development
- Small business

1. Behaviours:
   - Frequent online shoppers
   - Engaged with blogging-related content on Facebook
   - Active bloggers or aspiring bloggers
   - Engaged with blogging tools and software

Note that this is just an example, and you may need to adjust the audience based on your specific niche, target market, and campaign goals. It's important to test and refine your audience over time to maximize the effectiveness of your Facebook advertising campaigns.

1. Choose the right advertising platform: Google Ads, Facebook Ads, Instagram Ads, and LinkedIn Ads are some popular advertising platforms that you can use to promote your blog. Each platform has its strengths and weaknesses, so choose the one that is most likely to reach your target audience.
2. Set your budget: Determine how much you will spend on advertising. You can start with a small budget and gradually increase it as you see results.
3. Create engaging ads: Create ads that catch the attention of your target audience. Use eye-catching images or videos and write compelling headlines and ad copy.
4. Use targeted keywords: Use keywords relevant to your blog content and target audience. This will help your ads appear in search results and reach people interested in your topic.
5. Monitor your results: Monitor your ad performance and adjust your strategy. Use analytics tools to track your traffic, conversions, and engagement.

Remember that paid advertising is just one way to drive traffic to your blog. You should also focus on creating high-quality content, optimizing your blog for search engines, and promoting your content on social media and other channels.

Your Traffic generation strategy

After reading a lot about traffic generation, I know it's overwhelming.

You might feel, What should I do the next moment? I publish a blog post. Could you give me a Crisp?

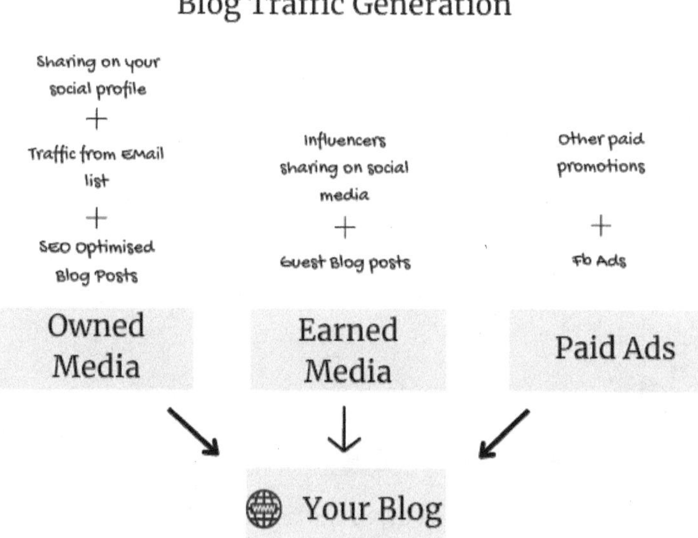

When you are getting started, You can't be everywhere. As you have seen in the learning ladder, You have much to learn and test. Start with one social platform of your choice. Say if you are good at creating videos, You can combine blogging and using youtube to generate traffic.

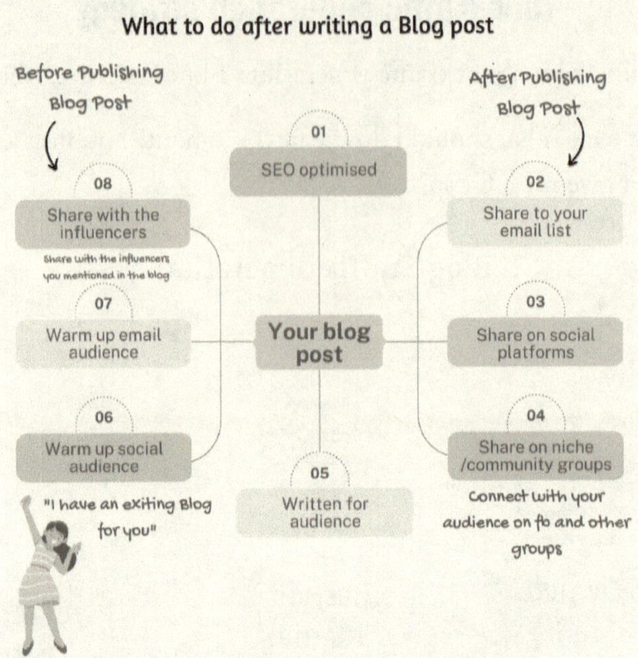

If you are good to go with Twitter, that's good. All I wanted is you to

1. Choose one social media to drive traffic-Your Primary Traffic Channel
2. The email list is the second traffic channel.

As you grow, you have a team and repurpose your content to expand your reach.

> ## Action Steps:
>
> 1. Define your one primary traffic source- Social media
> 2. Create lead magnets.
> 3. Create landing page for your lead magents.
> 4. Build your email list from day 1.

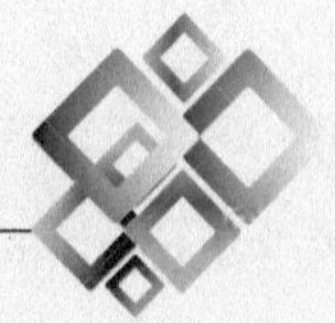

CHAPTER 9

REVENUE GENERATION

$\mathcal{B}$log monetization is like planting a seed and tending to a garden. Just as a seed needs the right soil, water, and sunlight to grow into a healthy plant, a blog needs the right monetization strategies to grow and thrive. As the blog's owner, you are the gardener, carefully selecting the right monetization methods and tending to them regularly to help your blog reach its full potential and bear fruit in the form of income. Just like a garden, a blog requires patience, effort, and persistence to thrive, but with the right approach, it can blossom into a bountiful source of income and fulfillment.

The chart shares the common reasons for starting a blog. **12.33% of people started a blog to make money, and most people 24.17% started blogging as their creative outlet.**

Remember the digital contract we created in chapter 3? My advice would be not to break the contract(the trust) with your audience for a short-term incentive. If you started a blog to

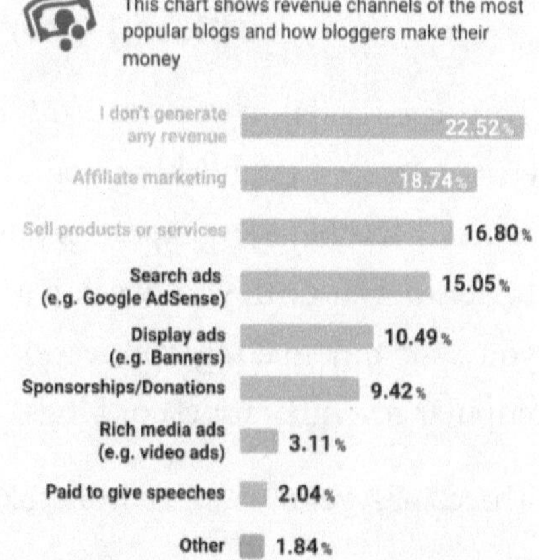

express your creativity and chose the wrong monetization method(or at the wrong time), looking at your fellow creators leads to a slippery slope.

Always stay focused on the long term.

With that thought in mind, to stay focused on a long-term benefit, I would like you to warn about certain things before we learn about the revenue generation models.

1. Not all monetization methods will work for everyone.
2. Only copy the Business model of others if it aligns with your strengths. For instance, if you are uncomfortable talking on camera- video course creation may lead to failure.
3. Always play to your strengths. If writing works well for you, Go with that! Monetize that skill and then learn the next skill. Don't jump from one skill to another just for the sake of learning and not earning.
4. Refrain from comparing your stage 0 with someone's stage 10. It leads to the wrong monetization path. Someone in your niche is selling courses, and memberships don't mean that you should create a course from day 1.
5. People buy premium and signature courses from the most reputed creators. Don't fall for High-ticket offer advice. When starting, building an audience and trust is more important than selling.

Finding your Middle Ground:

Trust is essential in any sale, so focus on building rapport with potential customers and establishing yourself as a trustworthy and knowledgeable expert. Most blogging experts say don't monetize when you are just starting; better to wait until you develop a readership. Your Middle ground where you stay and making connections with your readers. Let's look at the popular revenue models of blogs.

There are several ways to monetize a blog:

1. **Advertising:** You can sell advertising space on your blog to businesses that want to reach your audience. You can use an ad network like AdSense or sell ad space directly to businesses.
2. **Affiliate marketing:** You can earn a commission by promoting other people's products on your blog and linking them with an affiliate link. You deserve a commission when someone clicks on the link and makes a purchase.
3. **Sponsored content:** You can work with brands to create sponsored content that promotes their products or services. You can either write the content yourself or have the brand provide it.
4. **Digital products:** If you have expertise in a particular area, you can create and sell digital products like ebooks, online courses, or printables.
5. **Services:** You can use your blog to promote your services, such as coaching, consulting, or freelance writing.
6. **Membership programs:** You can create a membership program where subscribers get access to exclusive content, discounts, and other perks in exchange for a monthly fee.
7. **Donations:** You can get donations for your content.

As you hover over different monetization models, consider how your audience views you. If they trust your opinion and feel great about the products you suggest, you can start with affiliate offers. If they trust your ability and expertise, you can begin with coaching or creating products. It is not a restrictive model but something to consider before you leap in. The method of revenue generation should combine with your goals and the realities of creating a product/content sometimes. How scalable they are, how much work is required, and the expected timeline to profit.

There are a lot of ways to reach the final line. For example, if your goal is to make ₹10,000/month, that could be selling,

- Ten courses at ₹1000

- 50 eBooks at ₹200
- 3 Sponsored posts of ₹3300
- 2 Consultation gigs at ₹5000
- 200 sales of an affiliate offer to return ₹50
- 20 subscriptions to your membership site at ₹500
- Or the combination of the above.
  So choosing your middle ground is essential. Ask yourself
- What is the current stage of your business(Refer learning ladder)?
- How much time can you spend on creating content or product?
- What skills do you have? or What are you planning to acquire?

Tailor-Made revenue model:

I have seen bloggers working day and night earning meagre. On the contrary, bloggers make handsome money in the first few months of getting started. Many bloggers try to make money by blogging, yet only a few succeed. <u>22% of bloggers are not at all making money.</u> There is a cold-hard truth behind this scenario.

Remember, we are talking about building a profitable blogging system, which means doing a real business. Not just publishing content for the sake. With that approach, I am here after considering the best possible revenue streams to build a business, not just money-making methods.

People don't monetize a business. It gets monetized naturally. Every business requires a central marketing hub - that's where the blogs get into the picture. The table below outlines different revenue streams and skills needed for that.

Revenue Model and their success factors

Revenue Model	Fits If	Skills Needed	Success Factor
Digital Products- EBooks, Templates, Printables, Workshe ets, audio files, videos, design files etc.	• You are comfortable turning your expertise into a product.	• Writing • Designing the products • Marketing the products** • Email list growth(lead generation)**	Find the existing Product gaps and create a product that is market fit.
Physical Products	• If your niche fits in selling the physical products.	• Same skills as of digital products.	Find the existing Product gaps and create a product that is market fi t.
Coaching	• If you are not camera conscious. Ready to create live/ group coaching or creating video courses. • If you are ready to spend on the tool stack.	• Same skills as of digital products + • Planning and creating a course structure • Effective presentation skills • Video creation • Video editing*	Uplifting the people. Your success is measured with the success of your attendees.

Workshops	• If you enjoy public speaking and expert enough to answer the audience online. • Not a camera conscious person.	• Same skills as of digital products + • Subject expertise • Live Answering capabilities • Usage of Tech tools(Zoom, CRM etc)	Giving immediate transformation for people. Ex: Lead generation workshop that helps people generate effective leads.
Offering Services	• If you are able to deal with businesses / 1:1 people. • If you like working behind the scenes to bring in transformation for people/ businesses.	• Finding clients and serve them in the best way • Effective communication skills • Excellent problem solving and providing creative	Creating a consistent lead generation system serves in a long run.
Membership site	• If you are content machine, who likes to write and ship effective content • Creative enough to provide excellent content(including audio, video and templates)	• Effective writing skills • Consistency in writing • Effective communication • Ability to deal large group of people • Not for people who cannot create consistent content.	Gated content that provides immense value and helps people effectively.

Affi liate Marketing	• If you can write content to promote others products. • If you are able to educate about the product to the people • For people who don't want to create their own products.	• Convince and promote the products • Building real relationship with people to survive in a long run. • Fits perfectly for beginners	Choosing the best products for the audience.
Sponsored Blog Content	• If you have a site with well established readership.	• Pitching blogs	Your content and your email list.
Ads	• For everyone who writes content.	• Beginner friendly revenue stream. • Writing and building readership	Choosing the best ad revenue network.
Donations	• If you are ready creating gated content	• Beginner friendly stream.	Choosing the best donation platform.

The groundwork you laid in the previous chapter is to get your blog ready to monetize. How do you monetize a blog? What will convert it into a business?

Successful bloggers follow a roadmap and understand the four essentials of building a blogging business.

1. Blogs don't make money; businesses do. Combining different revenue streams lets you turn your blog into a business.
2. Money is on the list- You make money by gaining customers.
3. Selling something is the best way to earn a customer.
4. To sell something, you need to gain their attention first - this is where your content gets into the picture.

Attention is the new currency!

It is the kind of business system you have seen everywhere. From <u>Amazon</u> to insurance to car dealerships- All the business models are built with customers as the base. In our scenario, an email list is the base of everything. That is why I added the list building in the skills needed column. Most people model their competitors or influencers in their niche. So if that person sells a premium course, you do the same. If that person is providing SEO service, you follow that. Modelling someone where you are getting started is acceptable, and it happens when you see a successful person.

But this also poses a hidden problem that most people must be aware of.

The way they make money will not necessarily work for you. Let's put it this way, Can everyone make money through the same method and same strategy? Moreover, look at these dangerous statements

1. Self Publish a book in One week.
2. A membership site is for everyone.
3. Anyone can create a course in 90 days.

Isn't it perilous for a beginner to create a course in 90 days? Even if you make it, will that be beneficial for the user? Before choosing your revenue model, consider your skill and blog growth stage. That's where the tailor-made revenue model fits in. When you maximize your skill, you bring out the best. Creating a video course is not your revenue model if you are camera conscious. On the other hand, if writing works well for you, creating a publication works best for you. Play to your strengths and do more of what's working for you. I have broken up these revenue streams level-wise. Have a look at the image below. Level 1 fits perfectly for beginners- You can spend more time building your audience than concentrating on selling. Levels 2 and 3 fit anyone who already has an established audience.

Most beginners hop into the level 3 revenue stream as their first offer. Will you spend $2000 on someone's premium course? Of course, yes! The condition is you should know that person well; You should have tasted the quality of his products. That is why beginning with level 3 is hard if you don't have an audience and expertise.

Revenue Streams

Your first product should not be a premium course, especially if you are new to marketing and selling. I didn't mean that you should not sell the premium course; you can have premium digital products but start with a small product. The mistake I made in creating my first product was to go with a full-fledged premium course. I fell into the trap of "You can create a premium course in 90 days." I also felt the pressure of creating and selling the course as the subject was Aeronautical(the technical things were heavy). At that time, I underestimated the time and resources that go into creating a complete premium course. I hated the process, as I was the only one outlining, scripting, shooting, editing and publishing the course. I didn't even outsource the process of creating landing pages and generating ads. The lesson here is to create a premium course only after you have tested a few or more small digital products.

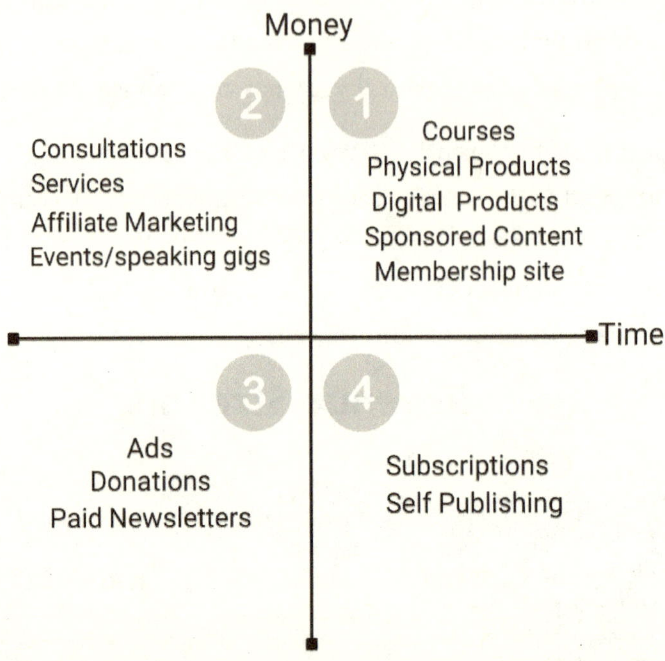

Time = the amount of time one required to create content/create product/acquire leads

When you start selling, learning the selling strategy is essential, not the product. Your first goal should be to give your audience a taste of your product. Once they understand and know about your paid product, there is a higher chance of them returning to you. That way, you can sell your premium course more quickly. This way, I am summing up this tailor-made revenue model to hit the milestone of the first $1000. The graph below shows you the monetization methods placed on the quadrants; time here means the time required to create content or create the product. In the case of donations as your revenue model, you don't need more time to create content to monetize. The methods in quadrant 1 require more time and generate more money. To hit your first $1000 revenue, you can combine multiple methods. You can use a combination of Ads + Affiliate Income + Service.

Say you are a web designer; you can sell your web design service to clients and monetize your content with ads and affiliate links.

As a coach, you can combine affiliate marketing and selling courses.

One of my students was an avid book reader; she started writing about self-help and productivity. Her writing is so mature, and her content helped many. The money she made with ads and affiliate income(Amazon links on books is as low as 3%) was very low. She approached me with a suggestion of changing her niche after she had gained 10,000 email subscribers. She wanted to introduce people to a new niche. But after a lengthy discussion, we devised an entirely different strategy. The strategy was to create and sell planners as her first product, and we tested it. It worked very well. This method of selling small products is termed as Tripwire funnel.

Creating a Tripwire Funnel:

A tripwire funnel is a strategy used in marketing and sales to convert visitors into customers by offering a low-cost, high-value product or service. The tripwire funnel aims to get the customer to make a small purchase or commit to a low-cost offer, which leads to an upsell or cross-sell of a more expensive product or service. A tripwire funnel aims to monetize the customer as quickly as possible while providing them with a valuable product or service to help them achieve their goals. This type of funnel works well when you have a targeted audience and your product or service is relevant and valuable to them.

Once you have a subscriber list or while building subscribers, you can make money through the tripwire products. Exceed nutrition does this well with its digital products for fitness coaches. Look at the lead magnet page below,

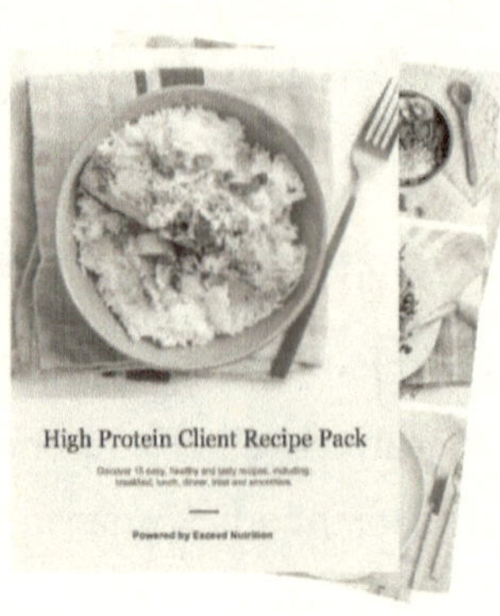

Free High Protein Client Recipe Pack To Help You Boost Brand Engagement & Client Results

Once people signup for their mailing list, they are redirected to the tripwire landing page, where they sell their white labelled book copies for a 50% discount. Look at the tripwire landing page below.

Claim your bonuses.
Get our white-label versions.

Bonus #1:	**Bonus #2:**
50% Discount Unlocked!	**50% Discount Unlocked!**
Vegetarian Recipe Pack: 58 deliciously healthy recipes that combine lacto-ovo vegetarian yumminess!	**Vegan:** 40 nutrient dense recipes to help your clients easily navigate a vegan lifestyle.

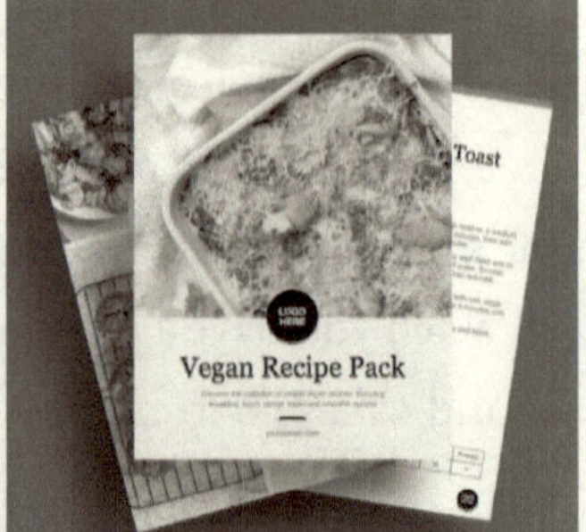

Offering a high-value product at a low cost may seem like something other than beneficial initially, but that leads you to sell your high-ticket offers. Here are the few tripwire products you can offer

- eBooks, Pdf Guides
- Printables
- Workbooks, Spreadsheets
- Mini Online courses
- Webinars
- Templates, Checklists
- Mockups
- Masterclasses
- Free trial of your products/service.

Mentorbox offers a three-day trial for $1. This way, people can see what the mentor box offers in its paid subscription. Likewise, you can choose a tripwire that suits you.

By now, you have a clear idea of building your tailor-made revenue model for your blog based on your time, skill and niche. Let's explore the different monetization options. I will show you an overview of other money-making methods from blogs and the pros and cons so that you have a clear picture of choosing a strategy for your blog.

Exploring Monetisation Methods:

Blogger reaps the reward of their hard work in the form of revenue. Most people here start with ads as their primary income stream. That approach is acceptable, but ads annoy and distract your readers. I don't recommend placing ads if you have an idea to sell your digital products. Instead, you can capture the audience's attention with your content. The quality of your content is the investment for building your business. With that simple tip, I will write about the pros and cons of monetizing methods.

Donations:

If you are someone working 9-5 and want to start your freelance business or consultations, getting started with donations is the easiest and quickest way of monetization. People are often happy to contribute directly to thank you for your work. Sites like Patreon and Buy me a coffee allow you to easily create pages and pop-ups that you can add to your articles or website. The idea here is you are prompting people once they have received value. Patreon and Buy me a coffee offers you to create membership levels and sell products. Just like the image below from the studio elan's page.

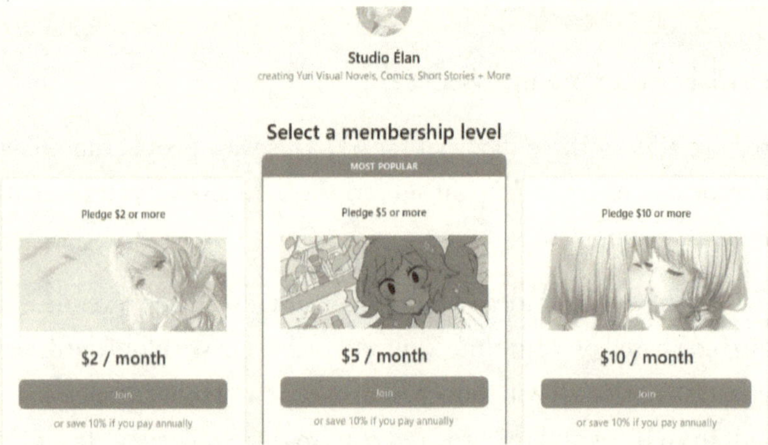

You can write articles and include your Patreon page link at the bottom and get monetized easily. If you are testing your idea of starting a membership site, this will help you a lot.

Pros:

1. Low barrier entry.
2. No need for technical knowledge to create pages or sites. You can directly start with the sites mentioned above
3. Beginner friendly.

Cons:

1. Not everyone is happy to offer donations.
2. Driving initial traction is challenging. It will help if you put more effort into getting traffic and building an audience.

Advertisements:

The next popular approach to monetization is, of course, advertisements. There are multiple ad networks that you can utilize for your site. Advertisements can negatively impact the user experience. Pop-ups, banner ads, and other types of advertisements can be disruptive and make it difficult for users to focus on the content. This could lead to a high bounce rate, hurting the blog's ranking and visibility. Here I am summing up the different ad networks and their pros and cons. Since ads can pay only $2 to $3 per thousand impressions(page views), Which indirectly means you need a lot of traffic to make $60 - $70 through ads.

You have probably heard of Google Adsense when monetizing a blog with ads. But I recommend something other than google adsense as it is hard to make money from it. You can signup for other ad networks like Mediavine or AdThrive. The Problem with Mediavine is they require minimum traffic to get started. Once you have established an audience, you can make handsome money with mediavine. As we focus more on building a profitable revenue stream for writing, advertisements can be an additional stream rather than the primary income stream.

Instead of these ad networks that take up a lot of space on your site, you can write sponsored posts and paid reviews.

Sponsored posts:

Sponsored posts mean a paid blog post by an advertiser. Brands looking for exposure will provide their product for review or feature in their post. In return, the blogger will feature the product in their post. An example of a sponsored post might be a beauty blogger reviewing a new skincare line on their blog and Instagram account. The skincare brand might provide you with a selection of products to test, as well as guidelines for the tone and content of the post. You can create a blog post with the photos of the products, detailed information about the ingredients, and their personal experience using the products. You can also include a discount code or a link to purchase the products online.

It's important to note that sponsored content should be disclosed to the audience per the guidelines set by the Federal Trade Commission (FTC) in the United States and similar regulatory bodies in other countries. The blogger or influencer should disclose that the post is sponsored and that they have received compensation for creating it.

Look at the sponsored post by <u>Spotify</u> on Buzzfeed below, a way of promoting their brand to a broad audience. <u>It provides content that many music lovers find exciting and contains a call to action to listen to the artists' music on Spotify.</u> As you can see, it is clearly mentioned as a paid post as per guidelines.

BuzzFeed   Quizzes   TV & Movies   Shopping   News   Tasty

Paid Post   Posted on Dec 31, 2013

15 Bands That Probably Wouldn't Exist Without Led Zeppelin

When the heavy-handed rockers reinvented the blues, they revamped rock music as we know it in the process. Here's a handful of modern-day music makers that owe signature parts of *their* sound to waves initially made throughout **Led Zeppelin's catalog** — now streaming in full on **Spotify**.

Spotify
Brand Publisher

To get a sponsored post, you can reach out to companies or brands they believe would be a good fit for their audience. You can do this by sending an email or direct message explaining your audience demographics, reach, and the type of content you produce. You should also include a media kit with your rates, statistics and examples of your previous sponsored content.

Paid Reviews:

You are getting paid directly by the advertisers to review their products on your blog. It's a grandchild of the sponsored post; you can sometimes get paid as money or the products.

Pros:

1. Easy to set up and beginner friendly.
2. Sponsored posts and paid reviews are more like blog posts and don't spoil your branding as ads do.

Cons:

1. Ads are annoying and distracting
2. Page load speed is affected
3. Sometimes it's challenging to get sponsored posts.
4. You cannot depend only on this method of income.

Affiliate Marketing:

The next on the line is affiliate marketing. You promote others' products and services; you get a percentage of their sale—some of the top sites like Nerd wallet and Bank Bazaar monetize using affiliate links. You don't have to concentrate on customers. All you have to do is to deliver traffic to the vendor sites.

How can you convince people to buy through your links?

Here I am including popular affiliate post types and their conversion models instead of concentrating on affiliate networks.

Product Reviews:

Writing a review for popular products and ranking them on google is one of the most common methods of making money. It's relatively easy and lucrative.

<u>Guiding tech</u> does this by writing list posts on several products and writing detailed product reviews.

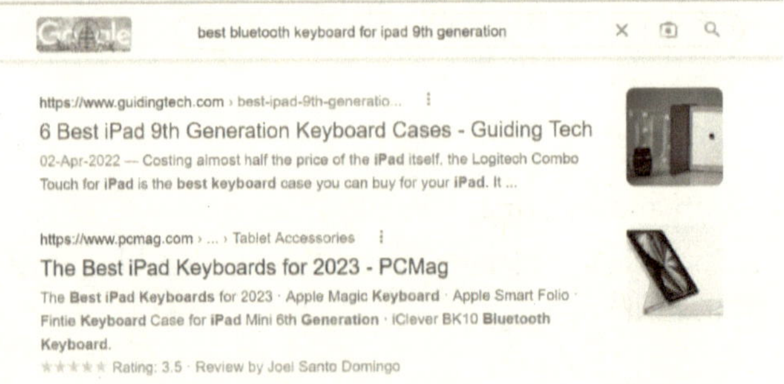

They focus on writing content that either reviews single products or multiple products. They link to them with affiliate links.

Finally, they optimize these pages for SEO to make them rank on Google for High Search volume keywords.

Hurray! That's all done from their end. Amazon pays them a commission for all the sales generated, and they get organic traffic from Google.

Email list marketing:

Another tactic for getting affiliate income is building an email list.

Once you have an email list and engage with them, you can promote products to those people.

Pros:

1. Lots of affiliate programs to choose
2. The review products will have low-competition keywords that are easy to rank.
3. Most people will be buyers, and there is a higher chance of a conversion.

Cons:

1. Your content needs to stand out. Too many niches are saturated, and people copy others' content.
2. It's challenging to manage the affiliate links, and you need a separate system for tracking that.

Products:

Physical Products:

Building your e-commerce store is one of the most challenging money-making methods. The real challenge is creating connections with making products and supplying them through suppliers. You have to set up a store on your blog and so on. It's a lot of work. But the results are fruitful.

I love Dr Hemapriya around here. Her site is one of the <u>top parenting blogs</u> in India. She writes about toddler nutrition, and the site ranks for multiple keywords. Her little moppet shop has multiple physical outlet stores and an online shop that sells baby nutrition products. When you explore the site, You can find that it is monetized with ads and few affiliate links. But the primary channel is selling products. This is how you can combine multiple income streams together.

Digital Products:

There are two different types of digital products you can create. They are information-based and Non- Information based. The Information products include eBooks, Guides, Templates, workbooks etc. The Non-Information products include Floor plans, Painting, Design templates, audio, video files etc.

The book you are reading is one of the information-based digital products.

There are a variety of digital products that bloggers can sell, depending on their niche and expertise. Here are a few examples:

1. **Ebooks:** Bloggers can write and sell ebooks on topics related to their niche. For example, a food blogger might write an ebook of their favourite recipes, while a finance blogger might write an ebook on budgeting tips. Take a look at <u>jagoinvestor.com</u>, selling ebooks on their blog.

2. **Printables:** Bloggers can create and sell digital printables, such as planners, worksheets, and templates. For example, a productivity blogger might create a printable daily planner, or a social media blogger might create a printable content calendar. The best example is <u>artsycraftsymom</u>, selling printables on her blog.

3. **Stock photos and graphics:** Bloggers who are skilled in photography or graphic design can sell their digital creations as stock photos, graphics, or templates. Ex: thedesignlove.com

4. **Audio or video content:** Bloggers can create and sell audio or video content, such as podcasts, webinars, or video courses.

5. **Apps or software:** Bloggers who have technical expertise can create and sell apps or software related to their niche.

6. **Templates:** Bloggers can sell digital templates, such as website templates or email templates, to help their readers create professional-looking websites or emails.

These are just a few examples of the digital products bloggers can sell.

Courses:

If you're keen on taking your monetization game to the next level beyond selling ebooks, offering online courses can be a lucrative option.

Typically comprising of video content that requires customers to sign in, online courses are perceived to hold greater value and can be priced higher than ebooks.

Pros:

1. Greater earning potential: Online courses are typically priced higher than ebooks, which can lead to greater earnings for course creators.
2. Establish authority: Creating an online course can help establish yourself as an authority in your niche or industry, leading to new opportunities.
3. Scalability: Once the course is created, it can be sold to unlimited students without requiring additional time or effort from the creator.
4. Flexibility: Online courses can be created and delivered on your schedule and at your own pace.

Cons:

1. Time-consuming: Creating a high-quality online course can be time-consuming and requires significant time and resources.

2. Technical challenges: Depending on the platform you use, creating an online course may require technical skills or the assistance of a developer.
3. Marketing: Creating a course is just the first step - marketing and promoting the course can be a significant challenge.
4. High expectations: Students who pay a premium price for an online course may have high expectations, which can lead to negative reviews if those expectations aren't met.

Membership sites:

If you are uncomfortable with selling an expensive course, then selling memberships may be a better option for you.

With this option, you can charge a monthly or yearly fee for access to premium content.

If it works for Netflix or Spotify, it can work for your blog too!

This is exactly <u>whatkidsstoppress.com</u> thought as well. They are a very popular parenting blog in India. They have a club membership; when people sign up, they get access to the monthly planned meal combo and recommend books for kids. Looking at their blog, you can see they have clubbed multiple monetization methods.

Pros:

- Offers a predictable source of recurring income
- Can create a loyal community around your blog
- Provides an opportunity to offer exclusive content or services to members
- Allows you to build stronger relationships with your audience
- Memberships can be customized to fit your specific niche or audience.

Cons:

- Requires time and effort to create valuable content and maintain the site
- Memberships may not be the best option for all bloggers or niches
- It may be difficult to attract new members and retain existing ones
- Can be challenging to balance free and exclusive content to appeal to both members and non-members
- Need to regularly update and refresh the site to keep members engaged and interested

Selling Services:

If selling a $50 course doesn't fit your need, You can start with selling services. Services include

- Freelance services.
- Consulting.
- One-on-one coaching or group coaching.
- Speaking Gigs.

Jyotsana Ramachandran from Happy Self-publishing is helping authors with curated solutions to publish their books. Apart from this, she is also training people to become authors through her online courses.

Pros:

- Directly use your skills and expertise to help others
- More control over pricing and project scope
- Potential for recurring clients and referrals

Cons:

- Limited scalability, as your time and availability are finite
- Can be challenging to balance service work with creating blog content
- Requires ongoing marketing and client acquisition efforts

I am happy if you aren't overwhelmed with the various monetization methods!

The whole idea of explaining various monetization methods, along with their pros and cons, is to show people how to choose a monetization method. Most people here replicate other successful creators without even accessing if it fits them. Now it's your turn to choose the one that fits you.

Building Your First Sales Funnel:

Simple and evergreen sales funnel. That is what we are going to learn.

A sales funnel is a series of steps or stages that a potential customer goes through before making a purchase. Every funnel should have a goal. The *way* you piece that funnel together has to serve that goal. There are many types of funnels that you can build depending on the product you are selling.

1. **Lead Magnet Funnel:** This type of funnel is designed to attract potential customers by offering them something of value in exchange for their contact information. The goal is to build an email list of interested prospects that can be nurtured with more targeted offers over time.

2. **Tripwire Funnel:** A tripwire funnel is designed to convert new subscribers into paying customers by offering them a low-priced, high-value offer immediately after they sign up. The goal is to create momentum and build trust with the customer so they are more likely to purchase additional products or services.

3. **Webinar Funnel:** A webinar funnel is designed to drive attendance to a live or recorded online event that provides valuable information to potential customers. The goal is to position the business as an authority in its niche and create a sense of urgency for attendees to take action at the end of the webinar.

4. **Product Launch Funnel:** A product launch funnel creates excitement and anticipation for a new product or service. The funnel includes a series of pre-launch content that builds anticipation and trust with potential customers, culminating in a launch-day promotion that encourages them to purchase.

5. **Application Funnel:** An application funnel is designed for businesses that sell high-ticket products or services that require a more personalized approach. The funnel includes an application process that qualifies potential customers and guides them through a sales conversation with a sales representative.

6. **High-Ticket Sales Funnel:** A high-ticket sales funnel is designed to sell expensive products or services requiring a longer sales cycle and higher trust-building. The funnel includes multiple touchpoints and personalized communication with potential customers to help them make an informed purchase decision.

Here's what a simple list-building funnel looks like:

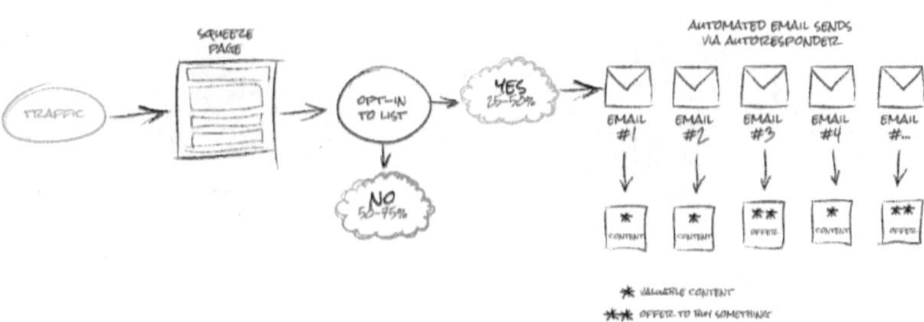

A person(Stranger) lands on your blog post, or the ad you created for your landing page have a look at the content.

Once he is satisfied with what you offer (a lead magnet may be an ebook, a free course, or a printable), he signs up for the ebook. That way, you get a subscriber.

Once you have their email id, you can build relationships/ promote your products or services.

That's how you turn a stranger into a subscriber. You can have a few more sequences like this to turn the subscriber into a buyer.

Let me explain that with the help of a Course Selling funnel. This includes a Webinar.

The webinar here acts as a gatekeeper to your course. You explain to people what they can gain from the course by teaching something valuable in the webinar. All you have to do is to drive traffic to the landing page. It may be organic traffic from SEO or social or from ads. Once people signup for the webinar, you can promote your paid course through email. The overall funnel looks like this.

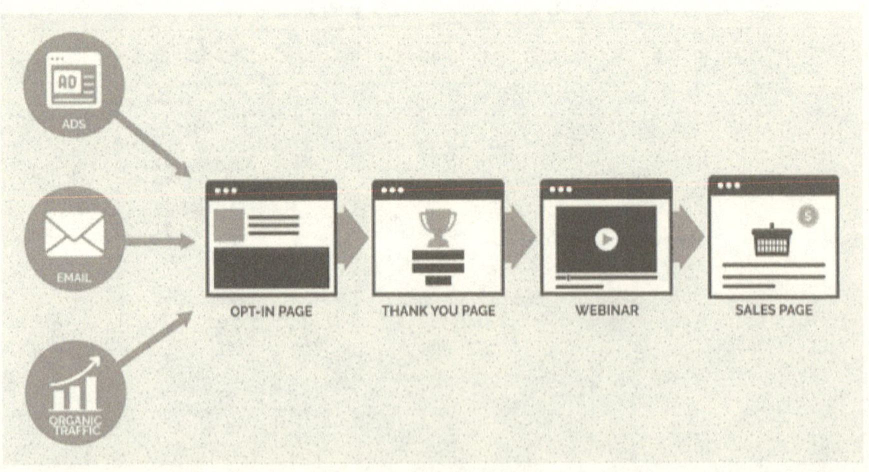

Steps to create a sales funnel:

You have a traffic source, which you send to the lead magnet landing page-that promotes the lead magnet.

Or, you have a traffic source which you send to a blog post, and the blog post has an opt-in form that promotes lead magnet.

In both cases, the lead magnet is a gateway to get your subscribers. Your priority should be on the lead magnet. So if that's wrong…

If that's something that isn't right for your business and offer…

You attract people who sit on your list and do nothing…

They don't buy.

They don't engage with your work.

You wonder, Do I have people on my list? So make sure you create an awesome lead magnet. What so ever it is. This is step 1 of the funnel.

Step 2: A landing page to capture the email address

Landing pages and opt-in forms serve an essential role in capturing your audience.

To do that effectively, landing pages and opt-in forms have to reflect the following:

- **The problem** the opt-in incentives hope to solve
- **Value** of the lead magnet to the reader
- **Potential outcomes** it has

The focus should be on the ideal reader. Here's the landing page sample.

Where can it go wrong?

When you focus on the features vs the benefits of what you're offering,

When you don't use words that resonate with your audience,

Or when what you're offering is not clear.

Tools that might help:

- Elementor
- Landing page templates from your email service provider will be an excellent go-to choice.
- Canva to create lead magnets.

Step 3: A email service provider to automate sales follow up

An email sequence is just a series of emails that inches your subscriber toward the end goal you've set for your funnel. The email sequence looks like this.

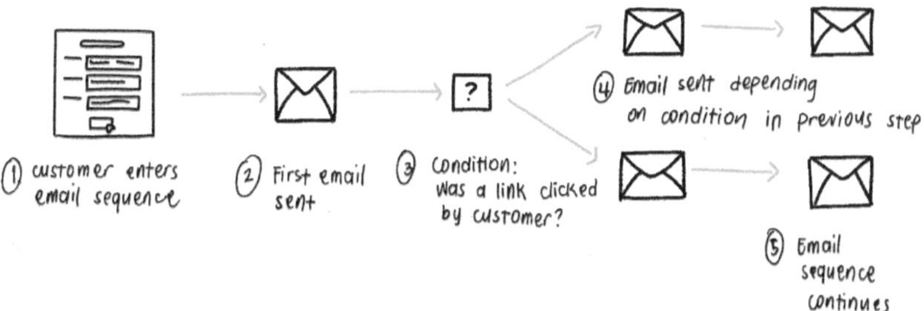

Once people are on the mailing list, you can create a series of emails to take them to your product landing page or buy the course/product.

Step 4: Setting up the sales page

A sales page has several sections.

Long-form or short-form.

Every section on the sales page must convince subscribers that your offer is for them.

If you have a solid sales sequence, half the job is already done by the time they arrive at your sales page.

This audience is already warm and needs a slight nudge. Nevertheless, your sales page has a few critical components that need to reflect the pain points that you made them aware of, get them to identify as someone who will benefit from your offer and share the benefits of your offer.

Here's an example of the different sections your sales page can have. Look at the sales page for <u>refactoring</u>. They have connected every piece together to let people buy the book.

Step 5: Collect payments through the payment processor

You're nearing the end of your evergreen funnel.

You are right here!

The easy option is to use woo-commerce and <u>RazorPay</u> or all-in-one services like <u>Sendowl.</u> The best way to receive Indian money is to go with Razorpay payment pages, or Instamojo is another alternative.

This is how you build a simple sales funnel.

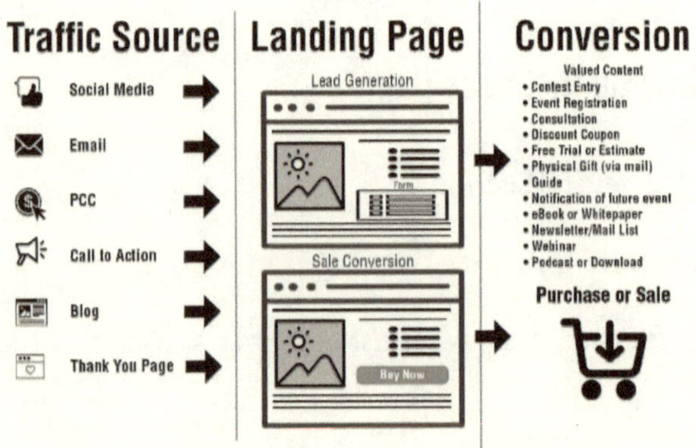

> ## Action Steps:
>
> 1. Plan your Monetisation method.
> 2. Start preparing the ground work for the method you choose. Ex: If selling ebook, then write a roadmap to sell.

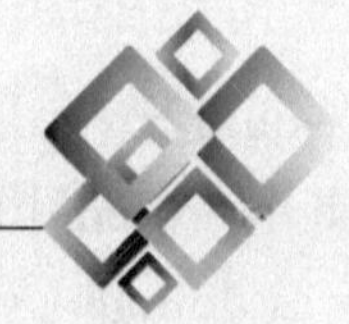

CHAPTER 10

THE PROFITABLE BLOGGING SYSTEM

*I*t's no secret that I love Blogging. It has changed my life. I have gone from not having a clue what a blog was, to having three successful blogs and a business that earns me good monthly money!

I get to earn a full-time income while being able to manage my family and be there when my kiddos need me. I get to call the shots, be my own boss and work the hours I want to.

BUT...

It has taken me the best part of 8 years to get here!

I want to go back and tell my beginner self everything I now know about starting a profitable blog. I could have gotten there sooner – with fewer mistakes and less stress!

Well, I might not be able to go back in time to help my beginner self – but I can undoubtedly help YOU!

That is why you are holding this book in your hands!

This book, about how to start a PROFITABLE blog in 2023, is the one I wish I had read back in May 2015 when I started my blogging journey.

It would have saved me so much time and meant I'd have started earning decent money from blogging sooner!

It would have also saved me A LOT of extra time not having to go back and fix stupid things I did in the beginning when I didn't have a clue what I was doing!! (And 8 years on, I am STILL fixing my newbie mistakes – seriously!)

If you're a beginner and you've made it this far, you might feel overwhelmed. It's normal to think that you have a lot to do and a lot to learn.

Let's summarise what you have learned into a 12 Month blog plan so that you set up and build a profitable blog from Day 1 and start building a business in one year.

The Overview of previous Chapters

- **Chapter 1:** Take the swot test and choose what type of blog you will start.
- **Chapter 2-** Identify your niche
- **Chapter 3-** Define what your blog is.
- **Chapter 4-** Purchase your Digital tech stack and setup.
- **Chapter 5** -Build Your rough content calendar(Refine this one after doing keyword research)
- **Chapter 6-** Do keyword research and determine what blog posts you are writing.
- **Chapter 7-** Write Blog posts
- **Chapter 8-** Decide what's your main traffic channel
- **Chapter 9 -** Plan how you are going to monetize your blog(This may change over time, get started with your idea)

I wrote the one-liner for each chapter, but I know how hard it is for a beginner to execute everything. This chapter is dedicated entirely to helping you execute the blogging tasks. How to plan, work and execute everyday tasks when working or doing this thing full time.

How to get started with blogging?

You may be wondering, after knowing all these things about blogging.

The very first task is to do the research.

What sort of research?

Not just doing a Google search, but analyzing how much time you have to do the work?

Fill in this,

I am ready to dedicate______________ hours/ per day to set up a blogging business.

The next step is to define your business goals.

Yes! It's business goals, not just blogging goals.

Knowing your goals can help you turn them into something quantifiable and measurable. This approach can help steer your blog in the right direction and ensure you stay on the right path. Without clear goals and a way to track progress, it's impossible to know if you're making progress.

Primary Goal: *Build a brand of authority in 12 months*

Secondary Goals: *Define what "Authority" is*

- *Grow monthly traffic to 30,000 visitors*
- *Get 300+ social shares and 10 comments per blog post*
- *Build email list to 20,000 people*
- *Increase email open rates to 20%, and Click through rate to 10%*
- *Grow customer base by 5%*

Have you noticed that each goal has a specific time frame and can be measured? The more precise and measurable your goals are, the better your chances of achieving them through your content strategy.

The metrics you track become a way to move towards these more essential goals systematically. Because they set a baseline and help you make decisions on priorities and focus over time.

These metrics typically fall into three buckets:

- **Traffic** (Owned, Organic, Social and earned)
- **Engagement** (Reading time, social shares, comments, inbound links, email open rate & click-through rate)
- **Leads & Growth** (Email subscribers, enquiries, webinar signups, customers, product purchases)

The pyramid blogging system you learn in the section will help you achieve your goals without selling your soul.

The Pyramid Blogging System:

Have you ever heard of the Egyptian pyramid?

- The Great Pyramid of Giza is the largest and most famous pyramid.
- It was built over 4,500 years ago and is estimated to have required the labour of over 100,000 workers.
- Pyramids were built as tombs for pharaohs and their consorts in ancient Egypt.

Ancient pharaohs needed a way to showcase their wealth and power to the world. The solution? Building towering pyramids that stood as a symbol of their authority and dominance.

But building a pyramid was a challenging feat. It took years of hard work, dedication, and a team of skilled craftsmen. Each stone was carefully selected and placed to create a structure that would stand the test of time.

Building a successful blog is like constructing a towering pyramid, brick by brick, layer by layer. Each blog post serves as a foundation stone, carefully selected and placed to support the weight of the content above it. With each new layer, the pyramid grows taller and more impressive, reaching towards the sky in a majestic display of skill and determination. The blocks must fit together seamlessly, creating a cohesive structure that draws the eye and commands attention.

But building a pyramid, like growing a blog, is about more than just the finished product. It's about the journey, the sweat and toil that goes into each and every brick. It's about the satisfaction of seeing your hard work pay off as your pyramid grows taller and more impressive each day.

"Failure to plan is planning to fail"?

The most prominent reasons I grew my blog into a success were a rigorous laser focus and a plan. **A month-by-month blog schedule that lets me focus and work towards my goal.**

Below is the profitable plan I followed at an elevated level to grow my first blog from 0 to over ₹30,000 per month in its first year. (I learnt this after three years of failure and figured it out.) Once I figured it out,

- In a year, I replaced my monthly salary.
- I worked in my spare time for a year, forgetting to binge-watch Netflix.
- In a year, blogging changed my life.

Just imagine how much your life will change a year from now. You won't get to ₹30,000 per month; maybe you'll go higher or only get to ₹3,000 monthly. That's not in the numbers but in the tasks you execute.

Here is the blog schedule and plan for the first year to grow your blog dramatically. I focused on three things

1. Grow an actionable Blog with great content
2. Build my email list
3. Create a digital product and launch it successfully.

When I wrote my goals, I chose digital products as my monetization method. Likewise, write your goal clearly with a well-defined monetization method.

Month 1: The Foundations- Start your Blog:

Your first month of blogging aims to lay the foundation for your blog. Get acquainted with the terminology of the blogging world, set up and personalize your site, and conduct research. This is the time to learn and be a beginner, and that's perfectly fine! Enjoy the excitement of being new, and don't hesitate to seek assistance.

We all begin with a blank blog and work our way up. Embrace the fact that you are embarking on a new journey. Use the 12-month blog plan to stay on track and organized, and let it be your guide as you progress. Download it from the resource library. I am including a 4 Month plan here(One Quarter). You can make use of the planner for the following months.

Tasks:

- Pick your niche
- Research other blogs in your niche- Make use of the workbook given along with the book
- Plan the structure and content for your blog.
- Define your creative edge.
- Choose a domain name.
- Before buying the domain name, make sure it's available on all social platforms. For ex: If your domain name Tot-o-Toddler, check if you have this available on social platforms too.
- Get a hosting
- Play with WordPress and themes. With tons of youtube tutorials, you can quickly learn to customize your blog.

- Choose your colour palette. Create a logo and favicon for your blog.
- Choose an email service provider.
- Define and start creating your Freebie. Use Canva, as it has ready-made templates to create lead magnets.
- Research Affiliate programs in your niche.

Tips:

Use these search operators to find the affiliate programs in your niche.

1. "Niche + affiliate program"
2. "Niche + partner program"
3. "Niche + affiliate marketing"
4. "Niche + affiliate network"
5. "Niche + referral program"
6. "Niche + commission-based program"
7. "Niche + monetization program"
8. "Niche + earn money online."
9. "Niche + make money online."
10. "Niche + revenue sharing program"

Make sure you record everything as you progress. This might help you in the long run.

The first month is where most people are struck with the shiny object syndrome. They think that no one will read the content when they don't have a well-optimized and designed blog. But once get past this and focus on content creation, you can, later on, optimize your blog the way you want as you grow.

Month 2:

In your second month of blogging, you should craft three remarkable pillar posts. By now, you should clearly understand your audience's pressing issues and concerns through your research. Write comprehensive and beneficial articles that help your audience overcome these challenges.

Before you embark on a writing spree, I implore you to have a specific intention behind each of your blog posts. As you continue to blog, you'll realize that there are numerous objectives you wish to achieve. These include increasing website traffic, expanding your email list, generating revenue, and more.

The image below shows you what type of blog posts to write and when.

Tasks:

- Build a writing habit. I suggest writing every day, even for 15 mins a day.
- Build your content calendar.
- Link your lead magnet to your pillar post and start sharing your blog post to drive traffic.
- Publish a minimum of 3 blog posts.
- Learn the writing process.

Month 3:

During the initial months of your blogging journey, concentrate on producing unique content, enlarging your email list, and promoting your posts. Don't stress too much about earning money at this stage, as it will eventually follow. Once you have established a solid blog, an active email list, and a decent traffic flow, monetization will become effortless.

The most challenging aspect of blogging is not the financial returns but consistently generating excellent content. Therefore, prioritize that task first; the money will eventually follow suit.

Tasks:

- Build a writing habit. I suggest writing every day, even for 15 mins a day.
- Follow your content publishing schedule.
- Promote your lead magnet on social media and start driving traffic.
- Write a List post or a roundup post to leverage other influencers.
- Learn to promote the blog on Pinterest; most niches work well with traffic.

In the first Quarter of your blogging journey, you should focus on sowing the seeds of knowledge and growth. Allow yourself to indulge in the joy of learning, as it is the foundation of your future success. Each day, dedicate yourself to one necessary action, setting up your blog or crafting a compelling post. Follow the Monthly Calendar Sheets to keep yourself on track and see your labour's fruit blossom into profitable progress. As you delve into writing, some blog posts take 8 hours to complete, while others can be finished in just one. Let your writing flow naturally, and know that practice will make perfect. On average, a blogger can craft ten blog posts monthly, each blooming with knowledge and creativity.

Month 4:

If you are writing every day, you know how to build readership. This month's focus is on building readership.

Tasks:

- Write emails- A weekly or monthly newsletter will connect with your audience.
- If you are more interested in building a social media community than an email newsletter, start building a FB group or Sub Reddit.
- Write blog posts supporting the pillar posts you created last month.
- Start product research; Analyse what product works well in your niche.

Overall, your first Quarter is building systems that push you daily. The overall blog growth plan looks like this. Building things one by one every day.

The Pyramid Blogging System

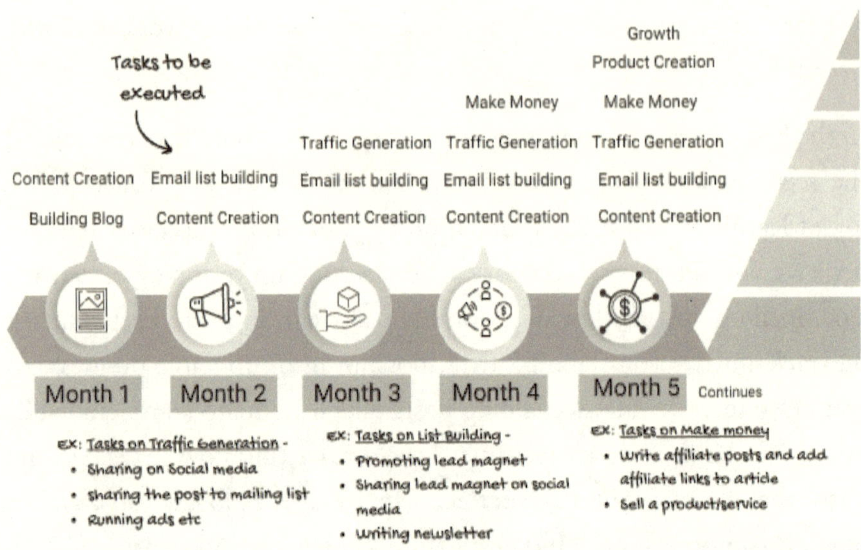

If you are ready to spend 2 hours daily, you can batch your work as in the image below. This is the schedule prepared by one of the boot camp attendees working 4 hours a day while caring for her family. To start, focus on completing one task per day. For example, you have too much to learn in the first month of getting started. Make a daily and monthly spreadsheet to plan and track your work.

If you are ready to spend 2 hours daily, you can batch your work as in the image below. This is the schedule prepared by one of the boot camp attendees working 4 hours a day while caring for her family. As we had planned these things so early, even before she started writing, she was so happy to see her blog take off as soon as in 8 months. It's not just the plan that has helped; her dedication and commitment towards it helped.

Tasks			
Month 1			
Hours	1	1	2	2
Week 1 Learning	Blog Setup	Content creation	Content creation
Week 2 Learning	Blog branding	Content creation	Content creation
Week 3 Learning	Content creation	Content creation	Content creation
Week 4 Learning	Content creation	Content creation	Content creation
Month 2			
Hours	1/2	1.5	2	2
Week 1 Learning	Content promotion	Content Creation	Content Creation
Week 2 Learning	Design email optin	Email list promotion	Content Creation
Week 3 Learning	Design freebie	Content Promotion	Content Creation
Week 4 Learning	Email list promotion	Content Promotion	Content Creation

As James Clear says,

You don't raise to the level of your goals; you fall to the level of your systems.

To sum up the first month goals are as simple as,

- Launching your blog,
- Publishing 10 blog posts,
- Getting an email provider,
- Creating your first email list and a freebie for that.

When you chunk the goals into tasks, you have few more things to concentrate on every month.

Things you need not worry about in the first Quarter:

- A minimalist and clear design is sufficient for your blog's aesthetics in the first month.
- Avoid adding flashy animations or spending time on a fancy tagline or description.
- Focus on creating engaging content that captivates your audience.
- Invest time in learning and growing rather than spending money on pricey tech tools, logos, or favicons.

Blogging Tasks an overview:

Here's a list of tasks for every blogger. Schedule these things in Google Calendar or any other time management tool you choose.

Daily tasks:

1. Check and respond to comments on your blog
2. Share your blog posts on social media platforms
3. Engage with your audience on social media by liking, commenting, and sharing other relevant content
4. Check your website's analytics to monitor your traffic and user engagement
5. Write and publish a new blog post or work on a draft of a future post
6. Research for future blog posts
7. Network with other bloggers in your niche
8. Check your email and respond to any inquiries or collaboration opportunities
9. Update your website and plugins if needed
10. Monitor and respond to any mentions or tags on social media

Weekly tasks:

1. Create a content calendar for the upcoming week/month
2. Write and publish a new blog post
3. Promote your latest blog post on social media platforms
4. Respond to any blog post comments or emails that require follow-up
5. Monitor your blog's analytics to evaluate the performance
6. Network with other bloggers or influencers in your niche
7. Work on improving your SEO by optimizing blog posts and website content
8. Update your blog's plugins and themes if needed
9. Participate in online communities related to your niche

10. Conduct outreach to promote your blog or collaborate with other bloggers or brands

Monthly tasks:

1. Evaluate your content strategy and make any necessary adjustments
2. Conduct keyword research and optimize your website and blog posts
3. Analyze your website's analytics to identify any areas of improvement
4. Update and repurpose old blog posts to increase their visibility and relevance
5. Plan and create content for the upcoming month
6. Monitor and adjust your social media strategy based on performance
7. Research and explore new marketing and promotion tactics
8. Collaborate with other bloggers or brands in your niche
9. Conduct an audit of your blog's design and user experience
10. Plan and launch any new products or services related to your blog.

In a day, if you have 2 hours to build your side hustle. Take 15 mins to execute the daily task. One hour to write content. Likewise, spend time meaningfully every day.

Blogging Tasks		
Growth	Managing	Connecting
Research for content	Designing your blog	Sharing your posts in fb groups and connecting with your readers
Writing content	Updating plugins	Communicating with influencers in your niche
Creating images	Replying Comments	Email outreach
Writing an email	Looking for new opportunities	Participating in group chats

Time management for Bloggers

Agree on it or not. We, as <u>humans, are limited in focusing our attention</u>. You can't have ten prioritized tasks. If you have so, then the word priority loses its meaning.

Managing time seems complicated at the beginning. When you master it, you are an intelligent person.

It is recommended to have top 3 priority every day and complete it.

Once you know how you waste your time, you can throw away those **time-consumers.**

Identify your time consumers, make a list of them and shut it down for some time.

How to make time to blog?

How do you find time to blog? I get this frequent question. The answer is that I make time to blog. I practice writing every day and managing tasks every day. The answer may be different for you.

The problem with managing time to blog is that we make ourselves enemies. It's true. Blogging is not a singular task. It's a multitasking job.

Multitasking is the enemy of productivity. Read about how <u>multitasking affects productivity</u>.

Prioritize the work:

If you sit at your computer without a plan, you will inevitably waste time.

You have to create a schedule and then stick to a schedule.

Life is full of distractions, understand that and stay focused while you work.

"Play while you play, work while you work."

How to prioritize the work?

Set Goals:

- Begin with defining the goals.
- Find out what you need to achieve the goal.
- Break down into tasks and group similar tasks.
- Bring the tasks into action.

Set a timer for every activity and try to complete it within the specified time.

Chrome extension: <u>Stay focused</u>

Android app I recommend: <u>tomato planner</u>

Batch working:

Grouping similar tasks is another time management technique. As a blogger, you can batch more activities than you can realize.

List of activities that can be worked in batches:

- **Keyword research:** While doing keyword research for one blog post, do it for three more blog posts. You can do this only if you have a content planner in advance. .
- **Writing blog posts:** When writing blog posts, prepare an outline for other blog posts in the series. If you find time, try completing two posts. You will feel like you have done something in advance.
- **Creating images:** I use <u>Canva</u> for creating images. I have a premade template for the social media images and pins. That saves a ton of time. I will go ahead with changing the background and headings. Ting! My image is ready.

A publishing schedule like this makes wonder,

Planning Your Publishing Schedule

Posting Frequency/No Of Posts	6 Months	12 Months
Weekly	1*26= 26 posts	1*52=52 Posts
Bi-weekly	2*26=48 Posts	2*52=104 Posts
Bi-Monthly	2*6=12 Posts	2*12=24 Posts

Blog Metrics you should measure:

As a blogger, analyzing your blog's performance is essential to understanding your audience, identifying areas for improvement, and optimizing your content and marketing strategies. This is where blog metric analysis comes in - it provides a quantitative way to measure the success of your blog and track your progress over time.

Methods to Measure Blog Metrics:

1. **Google Analytics:** One of the most powerful tools for analyzing blog metrics. It offers a comprehensive range of data, including pageviews, unique visitors, bounce rate, session duration, and much more.
2. **Social Media Metrics:** Most social media platforms provide built-in analytics tools to track engagement, reach, and other important metrics for your blog's social media accounts.
3. **Email Metrics:** Email marketing platforms offer detailed metrics such as open rate, click-through rate, and unsubscribe rate, which can be used to track the effectiveness of your email campaigns.
4. **SEO Metrics:** Several tools are available to track your blog's SEO performance, including Google Search Console, SEMrush, Ahrefs,

and Ubersuggest. These tools can help you track your search rankings, identify keyword opportunities, and monitor your backlink profile.

Essential Metrics to Measure:

1. **Traffic:** Traffic refers to the number of visitors to your blog. This metric can be broken down into various parameters: daily, weekly, monthly, or yearly.

2. **Pageviews:** Pageviews refer to the number of times a page on your blog has been viewed, including multiple views from the same user.

3. **Bounce Rate:** The bounce rate measures the percentage of visitors who leave your website after visiting only one page. A high bounce rate can indicate that your website may need some improvements.

4. **Session Duration:** Session duration measures the amount of time a user spends on your website, which can indicate user engagement and interest.

5. **Click-Through Rate (CTR):** CTR measures the percentage of users who click on a link, button or call to action (CTA) on your blog post or website.

6. **Conversion Rate:** Conversion rate measures the percentage of users who complete a specific action on your blog, such as subscribing to your newsletter, downloading a lead magnet or making a purchase.

7. **Social Media Engagement:** Social media engagement refers to the number of likes, comments, shares, and clicks on your social media posts related to your blog.

8. **Email List Growth:** Email list growth measures the number of new subscribers to your email list, which is a key metric for building relationships and promoting your blog to your audience.

Creating a dashboard record of these things will help you progress, or You can purchase my blog planner to help you get started.

Overall, you got the crisp of building a profitable Blog.

You now have everything to start a successful blog.

You have the learning ladder, the month-wise blog plan, the Keyword research process and the content creation idea to turn a blog into a business.

You may be whizzing about the ideas that run through your mind or disappointed about the things you missed. No matter what runs in your mind, you always have to fight that demon and push forward.

- Will people read my blog?
- They have already published the same content!
- Is blogging worth investing in?
- Will people buy my products?
- Will they signup for my mailing list?
- What happens if no one purchases?
- How will I end up?

All these questions have been screaming inside my mind for the past eight years. I am sure you will have these in a modulated tone and voice!

All I could say is

Push in forward. Bring traffic and test what you have learnt! That's the only solution. No feedback from your friends will help you.

Not just making money and growing a team will make a business successful. Your entire vision behind building the business is the catalyst for success.

Building a blogging business is a marathon; you must discipline yourself to balance work and life. That is a challenging task. With continuous effort and focus towards achieving goals, you will succeed for sure.

Before You wind up reading this book, make sure to download "The Profitable Blogger's Vault". That contains dozens of free workbooks and guides to establish a great blog. https://profitablebloggingsystem. com/bonus.

Good Luck, and Thank you for sharing your work with this world!

TOOLS I USE AND RECOMMEND:

Themes:

- Thrive suite
- Generate Press
- Astra
- Avada

Page Builders:

- Elementor
- Thrive architect,
- Divi

Hosting:

- Hostinger
- Cloudways

Chrome Extensions:

- Evernote Web Clipper
- Pocket
- Grammarly
- Google Analytics Debugger
- Check My Links
- MozBar
- Loom
- Canva
- ColorZilla

- OneTab
- Keywords Everywhere
- Notion web clipper
- Hunter
- Bitly
- LastPass

Payment Gateways:

- Woo commerce
- Razorpay
- Instamojo
- Paypal
- Stripe

Plugins:

- Rank math
- WP-Rocket
- Google site kit
- wp smush
- Pretty links

Email service providers:

- Mailchimp
- Mailerlite
- Convertkit

- Thrive leads
- Optin monster

Images editing tools:

- Canva
- Adobe tools

Writing:

- Grammarly
- Pro Writing aid
- Hemingway app
- Google Docs
- Ms-Word
- Portent content idea generator
- Coschedule headline analyser

Project Management:

- Trello
- Notion

SEO tools:

- Google Search Console
- Ahrefs
- SEMrush
- Google Analytics
- Ubersuggest
- Answer The Public
- Also asked

ABOUT THE AUTHOR

$\mathcal{H}$i! I am Durga Thiyagarajan. If you made it this far, Thank you so much for reading. I hope you enjoyed reading and learned at least one new thing.

If you are curious about how I ended up here- writing to you- here's my life in a crisp.

"If someone **eight years ago told me you would be an Entrepreneur earning from home, enjoying kids**, and running a family, *my eye roll would have been loud*".

So how did it all happen?

I started my journey as an Aeronautical Engineer, working with National Aerospace Laboratory and Quest Global. To this day, I love working with problems on aeroplane wings, aerodynamics, Bernoulli's theorem and much more to write. So I started with teaching online (Aeronautical subjects) to people writing the GATE exam.

Working full-time and doing this passionate teaching showed me a new path of building a side hustle.

And I continued teaching online even after my marriage. In 2016, only Skype and google classroom was the only option for teaching online.

I started a blog on Aeronautical, where I shared the study materials for free. I know nothing about lead generation or building an email list at that time. I started learning digital marketing from Digital Vidya to grow that blog and got certified as a digital marketer. This was my first step towards turning teaching into a full-fledged online business.

As the family grew, I spent most time pampering my son and little time teaching. I knew I had to make a change to continue doing what I love. I started writing niche blogs and worked with Digixlabs, a leading web design agency, to write for their clients. And guess what? Over the past five years, I have written almost every day for at least 3 hours, turning my passion into a profitable business.

I turned this everyday experience into a remarkable document in your hands!

Starting a blog can seem daunting, but with the right mindset and dedication, it can be a gratifying experience.

Thank you so much for reading! If you have any questions about the contents of this book, feel free to reach

out to me at durga@durgathiyagarajan.in or DM me on Instagram.

www.durgathiyagarajan.in

 **Before you go download "The Pro Blogger's Vault" from https://profitablebloggingsystem.com/bonus.**

This includes every resource I included in the book.

BIBLIOGRAPHY

1. Tumblr hosts over 518 million blogs, while WordPress hosts over 60 million blogs. https://ahrefs.com/blog/blogging-statistics/#:~:text=Internet users in the U.S.,the internet (W3 Tech).

2. 2.33% of bloggers don't earn any money at all. https://ahrefs.com/blog/blogging-statistics/#:~:text=Internet users in the U.S.,the internet (W3 Tech).

3. Learning curve models and examples https://www.valamis.com/hub/learning-curve

4. The Bumpy learning curve model - https://sascha-kasper.com/the-bumpy-learning-curve/

5. You grow girl - https://www.yougrowgirl.com/about/

6. This is Marketing by Seth Godin.

7. There are over 1.5 billion websites today. https://www.internetlivestats.com/total-number-of-websites/

8. Google processes over 40,000 search queries every second. https://www.internetlivestats.com/google-search-statistics/

9. The number of bloggers in the US is expected to grow to 31.7 Million. https://optinmonster.com/blogging-statistics/

10. Netflix has produced over 1,500 original titles. https://www.comparitech.com/blog/vpn-privacy/netflix-statistics-facts-figures/#:~:text=Netflix has over 17%2C000 titles globally as of October 2022

11. As there are 50,000 active blogs today. https://www.socialsamosa. com/2016/02/evolution-food-blogging-social-media/#:~: text=Food blogging is big!,food blogs out there today.

12. TikTok outranked its competition https://thedigitalmarketer.news/ organic-search/are-tiktok-eating-youtube-in-googles-results/

13. Look at the answers from quora for the above question https://www. quora.com/Is-blogging-going-to-be-dead-in-2023.

14. Labnol.org- https://www.labnol.org/

15. Yourstory.com-https://yourstory.com/

16. Shoutmeloud.com-https://www.shoutmeloud.com/

17. Sheer raise in the volume of bloggers https://serpwatch.io/blog/ blogging-statistics/#:~:text=6.7 million people in India,has an impressive blogging scene.

18. Mylittlemoppet.com-https://www.mylittlemoppet.com/

19. Subreddit tool -https://anvaka.github.io/

20. There are several reasons for the failure of 3D TVs**.**https://www. lifewire.com/why-3d-tv-died-4126776

21. A meaningful specific beats a wandering generality. An inch wide and a mile deep. Most people earning over $50,000 annually from blogging say they focus on a particular group. https://growthbadger. com/blog-statistics/

22. she corporated.com -https://www.shecorporated.com/

23. **73% of bloggers** who earn over $50,000 per year say they focus their content on the interests of a very specific group**.**https:// growthbadger.com/blog-statistics/

24. Value of Focus- Illustration by Milanicreative https://www.instagram. com/p/ClgFaU0M9mm/?igshid=YmMyMTA2M2Y%3D

25. ****2501+ Best Blog Names Suggestions And Ideas-https:// thebrandboy.com/best-blog-names/

26. Social Samosa Enables Industry by Leading Thought and Influencing the Influencers-https://www.socialsamosa.com/about/

27. **44% of buyers27** say they typically consume three to five pieces of content before engaging with a vendor. https://ahrefs.com/blog/blogging-statistics/

28. How google works image - https://www.quora.com/How-does-Google-crawlers-exactly-work

29. https://ahrefs.com/seo/glossary/short-tail-keywords

30. My Audience is Instagrammers who always seek ways to beat the Instagram algorithm.

31. A year since TikTok ban, Indian TikTokers narrate how their lives were https://www.indiatoday.in/technology/features/story/a-year-since-tiktok-ban-indian-tiktokers-narrate-how-their-lives-were-impacted-1823024-2021-07-02

32. Using keywords in a blog post, https://www.wordstream.com/blog/ws/2014/08/14/increase-traffic-to-my-website

33. Image - Simple email funnel - https://www.autogrow.co/how-to-create-your-first-email-sales-funnel-in-less-than-three-hours/

34. Simple webinar funnel image -[https://blog.hubspot.com/sales/sell-online-course-webina](https://blog.hubspot.com/sales/sell-online-course-webinar)r